FOOD WITH A VIEW

Food With A View

*Recipes from
Dudley's Restaurant
Snowmass Ski Area, Colorado*

PATTI DUDLEY

Copyright © 1993 by Patti Dudley

No part of this book may be reproduced in whole or in part, except for brief reviews, without written permission.

DUDLEY PRESS

First Printing 1993

Cover art by M.J. Commerford
Illustrations by Lea Mowan
Cover Design by Tammy Lane

ISBN 0-9638272-0-0
Printed in the U.S.A.

Food With A View

ACKNOWLEDGMENTS

Many thanks to our loyal customers and employees who have made our restaurant a success, and whose creativity and feedback have helped improve our food over the years.

Special thanks to the following people for their hands-on help, advice and support:

Peggy and Harry Mueller
Glenda Farnum
Tim McGinley
Jill Sheeley
Greg DeJulio
Tom and Janine Lake
my husband, Paul

Food With A View

TABLE OF CONTENTS

INTRODUCTION 9

ALTITUDE ADJUSTMENTS 11

CUT THE FAT 13

BREAKFAST 15

APPETIZERS 23

SOUPS 31

BREADS AND MUFFINS 47

DRESSINGS, SAUCES AND CONDIMENTS 67

SALADS AND SIDE DISHES 77

ENTREES 93

COOKIES AND BARS 131

DESSERTS 145

INDEX 181

Food With A View

INTRODUCTION

This book is the result of more than a decade of serving the valley's locals and visitors alike, first at our Airport Business Center location (as Dudley's Diner), and now on Sam's Knob at the Snowmass Ski Area. At Dudley's, you'll find not only great food, but unrivaled views of Mt. Daly, Garrett Peak and the Snowmass Valley.

With recipes ranging from simple to sophisticated, and healthy to indulgent, I have tried to make this is a cookbook for everyone. Use the recipes as a basis for your own creativity. Feel free to substitute or add ingredients that sound good to you. After all, that's how most of these recipes evolved.

As a result of my passion for baking, the dessert chapter is quite large, as is our display of tempting sweets at the restaurant. All recipes have been written for Snowmass' altitude, but are easily adjusted for lower altitudes. See page 11 before you begin baking.

If you've eaten at Dudley's, now you can enjoy your favorite dishes at home. If you haven't visited us, my hope is that the recipes in this book will convince you to. Let us do the work! We're located at the top of Lift #3, at 10,630 feet in elevation, where the views are possibly the best in Snowmass.

Food With A View

ALTITUDE ADJUSTMENTS

All recipes in this book were written and tested for high altitude. The only recipes that need to be adjusted for lower elevations (below 6,000 feet) are those recipes calling for baking soda or baking powder.

Make the following simple adjustments to cookie, dessert and muffin recipes:

—Increase each teaspoon of baking powder and baking soda by ¼ teaspoon.

—Increase each cup of sugar by ⅛ cup.

Food With A View

CUT THE FAT

As we become more aware of the effects of fat, cholesterol, salt, and sugar in our diets, we begin to focus on leaner, lighter, heart-healthy recipes and ingredients. Below are some guidelines for modifying recipes and changing your shopping habits to meet your goals for healthy eating. As you learn to cut fat, it will become second nature.

- Instead of butter or oil, try cooking sprays, or use a small amount of broth for sautéing.
- Learn to use lemon juice, garlic and herbs for flavor, while cutting some oil out of recipes.
- Buy lean cuts of meat and trim all fat. Remove skin from poultry before cooking.
- Substitute nonfat yogurt for mayonnaise or sour cream.
- Instead of using whipping cream in a sauce, use a mixture of 1 cup skim or 2% milk with 1 tablespoon cornstarch mixed in. Cook until thick.
- Try some of the fat free cheeses now on the market.
- Use cooked, pureéd vegetables or fruit to thicken sauces and soups.
- Recipes calling for whole eggs will sometimes work with just egg whites. Experiment.
- When using oil, use olive or safflower oil.
- Do not overcook vegetables. They are the most nutritious when cooked al dente, or eaten raw.
- Use mustard in place of butter, mayonnaise, or dressing.
- Serve plenty of whole grains and beans to increase your fiber intake.
- Avoid processed foods with a lot of sodium. Stick to fresh, raw ingredients whenever possible.

Breakfast

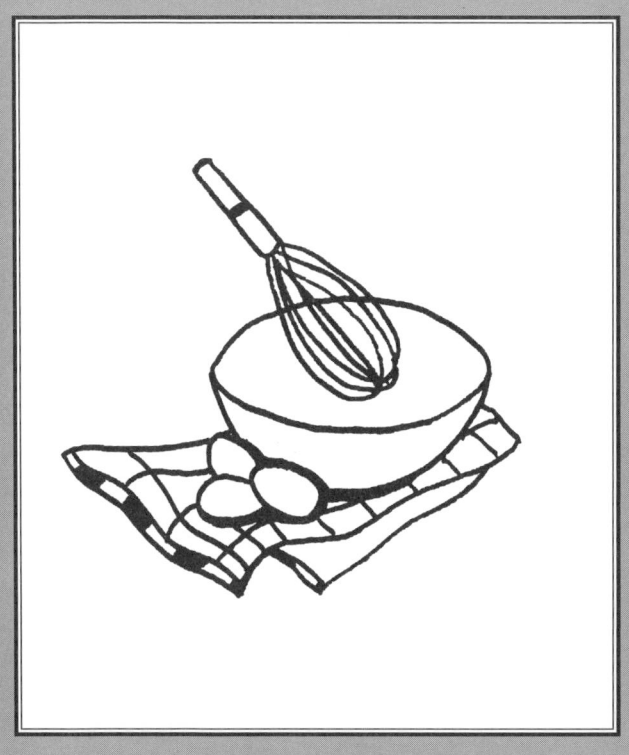

Breakfast

FRUIT SMOOTHIES

Serves 4

2 peaches
16 strawberries
2 bananas
2 tablespoons smooth peanut butter
1½ cups plain yogurt
1½ cups orange juice
¼ cup nonfat dry milk

Peel the bananas and place in a blender. Cut the peaches in half, remove the pits and add to the blender. Remove hulls from the strawberries and add. Add all remaining ingredients and blend well.

You can vary the types of fruit you use for these smoothies. If fresh peaches or strawberries aren't available, use frozen, but thaw them first.

Breakfast

BREAKFAST BURRITOS

Serves 4

6 eggs
2 tablespoons half & half
butter for frying
8 strips bacon, cooked and crumbled
¾ cup shredded cheddar or jack cheese
½ cup salsa (see index)
4 flour tortillas, warmed (see index for homemade)

Whisk the eggs and half & half in a bowl. Preheat a 6" non-stick skillet. Melt a small amount of butter, or use a non-stick spray for frying. Pour in one forth of the eggs. There should be just a thin layer of eggs. Sprinkle with bacon and cheese, and spoon a little salsa down the middle. With a spatula, roll it up and cook just until set. Place on a warm tortilla and roll up. Keep warm while you continue with the rest of the ingredients. We serve these wrapped in foil so they can be eaten on the go, but you can serve them on a plate with rice and beans and additional salsa, if desired.

Each day on my way to work I would look around me and wonder. On both sides tall pines and aspens would glide by me. Below were freshly groomed ski slopes inviting me to be the first one down. When I arrived at the end of my commute, a million-dollar view of majestic peaks would greet me. And to think I could be stuck down below on a busy highway, commuting like so many others. No way!

-Fran Suiter

Breakfast

WHEAT SOURDOUGH PANCAKES

For a whole grain pancake, this one is remarkably light. However, feel free to use white flour in the cakes and in your starter.

Serves 4

1 cup starter (see index)
2 cups milk
2 cups whole wheat pastry flour
2 eggs
2 tablespoons sugar
¾ teaspoon salt
1½ teaspoons baking soda
3 tablespoons melted butter
butter and maple syrup

The night before you want to serve the pancakes, mix the starter, milk and flour in a non-metal bowl. Cover and let sit at room temperature overnight. In the morning, return 1 cup of batter to your starter. To the remaining batter, add the eggs, sugar, salt, soda and butter. Stir lightly. Depending on the consistency of your starter, you may need an additional tablespoon of flour. Try one cake first.

In a preheated, lightly buttered skillet, drop batter to form small pancakes (3"). Cook until bubbles appear. Turn cakes and finish cooking.

Serve with butter and warm maple syrup.

Breakfast

DUDLEY'S HUEVOS

Serves 6

12 eggs
½ cup half & half
1 cup canned diced green chiles
½ lb. grated cheddar or jack cheese
12 flour tortillas
1 recipe Green Sauce (see index)
sour cream and green onions for garnish

Warm half the tortillas by wrapping in a damp towel and microwaving for 30 seconds.

Whisk together the eggs and half & half. In a non-stick skillet, scramble the eggs in butter until almost set. Mix in chiles and cheese, and finish cooking. Divide between the 6 warm tortillas, roll up, and place on plates. Smother in green sauce, or salsa. Garnish with sour cream and green onions. Warm remaining tortillas to serve on the side.

Campground Trail was named after the Forest Service campground that used to be located at the bottom. The long flat area of the trail is named Tee Pee Flats from the tour days when the timber was stacked up in piles that looked like an Indian village. The pitch after the flat is named Forest Fire Pitch because of a fire there when the trail was being cleared.

Breakfast

BUTTERMILK PANCAKES

These are thin pancakes, crisp around the edges.

Yield: 12 pancakes

¾ cup whole milk
¾ cup buttermilk
2 eggs
2 tablespoons sugar
3 tablespoons melted butter
1½ cups flour
¼ teaspoon salt
¾ teaspoon baking soda
¾ teaspoon baking powder
butter and maple syrup

Whisk together first 5 ingredients. In a separate bowl, combine remaining ingredients, then add to the milk mixture and whisk until all lumps are incorporated. Spoon onto a greased preheated griddle or pan and cook until bubbles appear. Flip and cook the other side. Serve with warm maple syrup and butter. Garnish with fresh fruit.

Breakfast

PACHOS

This is our breakfast version of nachos, made with potatoes and any assortment of vegetables on hand. It is often served with a fried egg on top.

Serves 4

2 tablespoons butter
½ cup sliced mushrooms
½ cup chopped green peppers
½ cup chopped green onions
2 large potatoes, cooked and diced
½ cup chopped fresh spinach
salt and pepper
1 cup shredded cheddar cheese
1 tomato, diced

Preheat broiler. In an ovenproof skillet, melt the butter. Add the mushrooms, green peppers, and green onions and cook 2-3 minutes. Add the diced potatoes and continue cooking until lightly browned. Stir in the spinach and cook 1 minute more. Season with salt and pepper to taste. Sprinkle with the shredded cheese, remove from the heat and place under the broiler until the cheese melts. Divide onto 4 plates. Garnish with diced tomatoes. Serve salsa on the side, if desired.

Breakfast

LOWFAT TURKEY SCRAMBLE

Serves 4

1 teaspoon olive oil
2 tablespoons sliced green onions
2 tablespoons diced green peppers
2 tablespoons diced red peppers
¼ cup sliced mushrooms
¼ cup cooked broccoli, chopped
¼ cup cooked turkey, diced
2 cups frozen egg substitute, thawed
2 tablespoons light cream cheese
4 tablespoons shredded lowfat cheese
¼ cup salsa

In a nonstick skillet, heat the olive oil. Add the onions, peppers and mushrooms and cook 2 to 3 minutes. Add the broccoli and turkey and stir for a minute. Pour in the egg substitute and cook, stirring, until almost set. Add the cheeses and cook on very low heat until the cheese melts. Dish out onto serving plates and spoon the salsa over the top.

Part of my job at Dudley's was to cut and display the desserts. Believe me, they are not to be missed! In fact, I recommend that everyone eat dessert first. You can always ski it off later.
                                            -Rachel Horvitz

Appetizers

Appetizers

GUACAMOLE

3 ripe avocados
1 teaspoon garlic salt
2 teaspoons fresh lemon juice
2 tablespoons chopped onion
1 teaspoon white pepper
dash of Tabasco or other hot sauce
2 tablespoons sour cream
3 tablespoons diced green chiles
Salsa (see index)
Tortillas for dipping

Mash avocados in a medium bowl. Add remaining ingredients and mix well. Season to your own taste. Serve with salsa and tortilla chips, or as an accompaniment to any Mexican dish.

Appetizers

CRAB TOASTS

Yield: approximately 60 rounds

8 ounces cream cheese, softened
2 tablespoons mayonnaise
2 tablespoons heavy cream
¼ cup diced onion
4 drops Tabasco
1 tablespoon sherry
½ lb. crabmeat
2 French baguettes
paprika

Preheat broiler.
In a medium bowl, combine first 6 ingredients and mix well. Set aside. Slice baguettes into ½ inch slices. Spread with crab mixture. Sprinkle with paprika. Broil until bubbly. Serve immediately.

Appetizers

BRUSCHETTA

Yield: 24 slices

1 12" French baguette
½ cup pesto sauce
2 oz. Montrachet goat cheese
1 cup sundried tomatoes, reconstituted and chopped

Preheat broiler. Slice baguette into ½ inch slices. Toast one side under broiler. Flip slices over. On the untoasted side, spread pesto sauce, then sprinkle with cheese and tomatoes. Return to broiler and broil until hot. Serve immediately.

Be creative and try other toppings, such as olives, sliced red onion, any kind of cheese or fresh herbs. The possibilities are endless.

Appetizers

CHILE CON QUESO

Serves 4

2 tablespoon butter
½ onion, diced
1 clove garlic, crushed
¼ teaspoon cumin
1 large tomato, diced
1 cup diced green chiles (roasted and peeled if using fresh)
½ lb. shredded jack or cheddar cheese
4 oz. cream cheese, softened
½ cup heavy cream
Tabasco and salt to taste
tortilla chips for dipping

In a medium saucepan, melt butter. Add onions and garlic and cook until onions are tender, about 5 minutes. Add cumin, tomato, and chiles and cook a few minutes until any liquid is cooked off. Add cheese, cream cheese, and cream. Carefully cook on the lowest heat setting until the cheese is melted. Season to taste with tabasco or any hot sauce, and salt.

Pour into a serving dish and garnish with tortilla chips and/or olives. Serve tortilla chips on the side for dipping, and salsa if desired.

Appetizers

NACHOS WITH BLACK BEANS

To make nachos into a meal, just add shredded chicken, beef, or seafood. Serves 4-6

Beans:
1 tablespoon oil
¼ cup chopped onion
1 clove garlic, diced
1 cup cooked black beans
¼ cup chopped green chiles
¼ teaspoon cumin
salt and pepper to taste

Nachos:
tortilla chips
½ cup diced green chiles
½ cup diced tomatoes
½ cup sliced black olives
2 cups shredded jack or cheddar cheese
1 cup guacamole (see index)
½ cup sour cream
salsa (see index)

For the beans, sauté the onions and garlic in the oil until soft. Add remaining ingredients and heat through. Mash the beans lightly as they cook, adding a little liquid if needed (from the can, or from the cooking liquid).

Preheat the broiler.
To assemble the nachos, arrange tortilla chips on a large ovenproof platter. Spoon the beans over, then the chiles, tomatoes, and olives. Sprinkle with the cheese. Broil until the cheese bubbles and begins to brown. Garnish with guacamole and sour cream and serve immediately. Pass salsa on the side.

Appetizers

SPICY SHRIMP WITH PEANUT SAUCE

Serves 8

1 pound shrimp, peeled and deveined, tails on

Sauce:
4 tablespoons peanut butter
2 tablespoons soy sauce
2 tablespoons water
1½ tablespoons rice vinegar
1 teaspoon sesame oil
1 clove garlic, crushed
1 teaspoon Chinese chili pureé

Seasoning Mix:
1 tablespoon paprika
½ teaspoon salt
½ teaspoon garlic powder
½ teaspoon onion powder
½ teaspoon cayenne pepper
¼ teaspoon black pepper
¼ teaspoon white pepper
¼ teaspoon thyme
¼ teaspoon oregano

Combine all sauce ingredients in a bowl and whisk until smooth. Pour into a dipping bowl and set aside.

Combine all seasoning ingredients and mix well. Sprinkle over shrimp and toss to coat. Broil or sauté shrimp just until done. Arrange on a bed of lettuce on a serving platter with the dipping sauce.

Appetizers

CARNIVAL CHICKEN

Serves 8

Curry Sauce:
¼ cup yogurt
¼ cup sour cream
2 teaspoons curry
2 tablespoons chutney

Banana Sauce:
1 banana, mashed
½ cup chutney
¼ cup orange juice
1 teaspoon curry

Jalapeño Sauce:
4 jalapeño peppers
¼ cup honey
1 tablespoon garlic
1 tablespoon cilantro
½ teaspoon cumin
1 tablespoon olive oil
2 tablespoons vinegar
1 cup lemon juice
1 tablespoon Dijon mustard

Spice rub:
3 tablespoons each: curry, cumin & cinnamon
2 tablespoons each: allspice, ginger, salt & pepper
1 tablespoon cayenne

4 boneless skinless chicken breasts

The 3 sauces may be made ahead of time. If you prefer, make just 1 or 2 sauces. For the curry and banana sauces, just combine all ingredients in a small bowl. For the jalapeño sauce, pureé the jalapeños, then add all remaining ingredients.

Combine the spice ingredients in a shallow dish. Cut the chicken into strips and dip into the spices to lightly coat. Broil or grill the chicken until just done. Serve with the dipping sauces.

Soups

Soups

CREAM OF ASPARAGUS SOUP

Serves 6-8

4 tablespoons butter
1 large yellow onion, diced
4 cloves garlic, chopped
5 cups vegetable or chicken stock
1 large potato, peeled and chopped
2 lbs. fresh asparagus
¼ cup fresh parsley, chopped
2 teaspoons dill weed
1 cup half & half
salt and pepper to taste

In a large pot, melt the butter. Sauté the onion and garlic until tender, about 20 minutes. Add the stock and the potatoes, and cook another 20 minutes. Trim the woody ends from the asparagus and discard. Chop the stems and add to the soup, reserving the tips. Continue cooking until the asparagus is tender, about 15 minutes. Pureé the soup in batches in a food processor or blender and return to the pot. Add the asparagus tips and herbs and cook 10 minutes. Add the half & half, and salt and pepper to taste.

The Big Burn was named because of a fire that burned across the area in the 1880's

Soups

VEGETARIAN LENTIL SOUP

If you're not a vegetarian, you may want to use chicken stock instead of the vegetable stock. If you don't have time to make the stock, use commercially available vegetable bouillon cubes.

Serves 8-10

1 cup lentils
6 cups vegetable stock
2 cups tomato juice
1 cup red wine
1 small onion, diced
2 cloves garlic, diced
1 medium potato, diced
1 carrot, diced
1 stalk celery, diced
1 cup sliced mushrooms
1½ cups chopped fresh spinach
1 medium tomato, diced
2 bay leaves
2 tablespoons chopped fresh parsley
salt and pepper to taste

Place lentils and vegetable stock in a large pot, bring to a boil, and simmer for 30 minutes. Add remaining ingredients and bring to a boil again. Reduce heat and simmer until all vegetables are tender. Add additional vegetable stock if the soup gets too thick. Season to taste with salt and pepper. This soup is just as delicious on the second day.

Soups

TORTILLA SOUP

Serves 6

2 tablespoons olive oil
1 medium onion, chopped
2 cloves garlic, minced
½ cup diced chiles (roasted and peeled if using fresh)
1 teaspoon chopped jalapeño chiles (optional)
2 tomatoes, diced
6 cups chicken broth
1½ cups cooked chicken meat, shredded
½ teaspoon cumin
salt and pepper to taste
3 corn tortillas
vegetable oil for frying
⅔ cup shredded cheddar or jack cheese

In a large pot, sauté the onion and garlic in the olive oil until soft. Add the chiles, tomato, and chicken broth and cook a few minutes. Meanwhile, cut the tortillas into ½ inch strips and fry them in ½ inch of oil in a skillet. Drain.

Add the chicken, cumin, salt, and pepper to the soup and heat through. To serve, place the tortilla strips in the bottom of the bowl, top with the soup, and garnish with the shredded cheese.

Soups

CHILE VERDE SOUP

Serves 6-8

2 tablespoons olive oil
1 lb. pork, cut into cubes
1 medium onion, diced
2 cloves garlic, crushed
6 cups chicken broth
1 cup pureéd tomatillos (optional)
3 cups diced green chiles
2 teaspoons diced jalapeños (optional)
1 cup diced canned tomatoes with juice
½ teaspoon cumin
8 tablespoons butter
8 tablespoons flour
1 tablespoon chopped cilantro
salt and pepper to taste
flour tortillas

In a large pot, heat the oil, then add the pork and sauté. Add the onion and garlic and continue cooking until the onion is soft. Add the next 6 ingredients, bring to a boil, then simmer until the pork is very tender, about 1 hour, or longer, depending on the cut of meat used. Add more chicken stock if needed.

Meanwhile, in a small saucepan, melt the butter. While whisking constantly, add the flour to create a roux. Cook on low heat, whisking, for 5 minutes. Add to the soup when the pork is tender. Cook the soup until it thickens. Stir in the cilantro, then season to taste with salt and pepper.

Serve with warm flour tortillas, homemade if possible (see index).

Soups

GAZPACHO

Serves 8

2½ cups canned crushed tomatoes
2½ cups canned diced tomatoes
2 cups water
1 cucumber, peeled, seeded and chopped
2 ribs celery, diced
½ cup chopped onion
½ cup diced green pepper
½ cup shredded carrot
1 tablespoon worcestershire
⅓ cup white wine
¼ cup vegetable oil
2 tablespoons lemon juice
¼ cup red wine vinegar
½ tablespoon Tabasco
½ teaspoon black pepper
1 teaspoon garlic salt

Combine all ingredients in a large bowl. Refrigerate several hours or overnight to let the flavors blend before serving. Serve chilled.

I love to see and talk to the foreign visitors from all over the world who ski at Snowmass and Aspen. Being from Switzerland, I always enjoy meeting people from home, and using my native language.

-Therese Kilchenmann

Soups

VEGETARIAN SPLIT PEA SOUP

This is by far our most popular vegetarian soup. Add ham if you like, but we prefer this version.

Serves 8

2 cups dry split peas
8 cups water or vegetable broth
1 cup chopped onion
1 cup chopped carrots
1 cup chopped celery
1 cup chopped potatoes
3 cloves garlic, crushed
2 bay leaves
¼ teaspoon liquid smoke flavor (optional)
½ teaspoon cumin
salt and pepper to taste

Soak the peas in enough water to cover; soak over night. Drain and rinse. In a large pot, combine peas and water and bring to a boil. Reduce heat and simmer one hour. Add onions, carrots, celery, potatoes, garlic, and bay leaves and continue cooking until peas and vegetables are tender, adding more water as needed.

Add remaining ingredients. Cook longer for a thicker soup, or add water for a thinner soup, depending on your preference.

Soups

CREAM OF MUSHROOM SOUP

Serves 6-8

3 tablespoons butter
4 green onions, chopped
1 lb. mushrooms, sliced
3 tablespoons flour
4 cups chicken or vegetable broth
2 cups half & half
2 tablespoons sherry
1 teaspoon dill
salt and white pepper to taste

In a large pot, melt butter. Sauté green onions and mushrooms for 5-10 minutes. Sprinkle flour over, and cook, stirring for 2-3 minutes. Slowly add remaining ingredients. Simmer 30 minutes. Adjust seasonings. This soup is actually better the second day!

Soups

POTATO CHEESE SOUP

Serves 6-8

4 tablespoons butter
1 medium onion, diced
1 clove garlic, crushed
3 large red potatoes, chopped
3 cups vegetable or chicken stock
1½ cups heavy cream
1 cup grated cheddar cheese
½ cup grated fresh Romano cheese
¼ cup chopped fresh parsley
salt and pepper
hot pepper sauce to taste

In a large pot, melt butter. Add onion and cook over medium heat until soft, about 10 minutes. Add garlic and cook 2 minutes. Add potatoes and stock, bring to an boil, then simmer 45 minutes, or until tender.

Pureé half the potato mixture in a food processor or blender, and return to the pot. Add remaining ingredients and heat through until all cheese is melted. Serve immediately.

Promenade was named for the promenading effect of the skiers under the lift.

Soups

CHICKEN-TORTELLINI SOUP

Serves 6-8

6 cups chicken broth
1 clove garlic, crushed
1 carrot, chopped
1 stalk celery, chopped
½ medium onion, diced
1 cup fresh spinach leaves, chopped
1 cup shredded, cooked chicken meat
1½ dozen frozen cheese tortellini
2 tablespoons fresh parsley
salt and pepper to taste

Place the first 5 ingredients in a large pot and bring to a boil. Cook until the vegetables are just tender. Add the spinach, chicken, and tortellini and cook 2 minutes. Add parsley and salt and pepper to taste. Serve immediately.

Soups

CREAM OF CHICKEN SOUP WITH GREEN CHILES

Serves 6

5 tablespoons butter
1 medium onion, diced
2 cloves garlic, crushed
4 tablespoons flour
3 cups chicken stock
1 cup diced green chilies
2 cups shredded cooked chicken meat
2 cups half & half
½ teaspoon cumin
1 tablespoon fresh cilantro, chopped
salt and white pepper

In large pot, sauté onions in butter until soft. Add garlic and cook 1 minute longer. Sprinkle flour over the onion mixture and cook, stirring, about 3 minutes. Add remaining ingredients and cook until thickened; do not boil. Season to taste with salt and pepper. Serve immediately.

Soups

CREAMY DIJON CHICKEN SOUP

Serves 6

1 tablespoon butter
1 cup chopped green onions
1½ cups sliced mushrooms
3 cloves garlic, chopped
3 cups chicken stock
3 tablespoons dijon mustard
½ cup white wine
1 teaspoon tarragon
1 chicken bouillon cube
6 tablespoons butter
6 tablespoons flour
2 cups shredded cooked chicken meat
2 cups half & half
salt and pepper

In a large pot, sauté the green onions in 1 tablespoon butter until tender. Add the mushrooms and garlic and cook a few minutes longer. Add stock, mustard, wine, tarragon and bouillon and bring to a simmer.

Meanwhile, in a small pan, melt the 6 tablespoons butter, then whisk in the flour and cook, whisking for 5 minutes. Add to the soup, then add the half & half and the chicken. Cook until thickened, then season to taste with salt and pepper.

Soups

SEAFOOD BISQUE

This is our most requested soup.

Serves 6

1 tablespoon olive oil
½ cup chopped green onions
½ lb. shrimp
½ lb. crab meat, flaked
1 cup chopped and seeded tomatoes
1 clove garlic, crushed
3 cups fish or seafood stock
1 bay leaf
1 teaspoon dill
½ tablespoon Tabasco or other hot sauce
¼ cup sherry
3 tablespoons butter
4 tablespoons flour
2 cups half & half
salt and pepper

In a large pot, sauté the onions in the olive oil. Add shrimp and cook until just pink. Add crab, tomatoes, stock, bay leaf, dill, Tabasco and sherry.

In a separate pan, melt the butter. Whisk in the flour and cook for 5 minutes. Whisk into the soup, add half & half and cook until thick. Season to taste with salt and pepper. Serve immediately.

Soups

VEGETARIAN CHILI

Serves 8

1 16 oz. can diced tomatoes, in juice or pureé
1 16 oz. can pinto beans
1 16 oz. can kidney beans
1 16 oz. can black beans
½ cup chopped onions
½ cup chopped green peppers
½ cup chopped celery
½ teaspoon Tabasco sauce
1 tablespoon chili powder
1 tablespoon cumin
2 teaspoons each: garlic salt, oregano, parsley
1 teaspoon coriander
1 teaspoon black pepper

Place everything in a large pot and simmer 1-2 hours. Serve with fresh bread or corn bread and tossed salad for a complete and healthy meal.

Soups

SAM'S KNOB CHILI

The flavor of this chili greatly improves after one day.

Serves 8

1 lb. ground beef
1 cup chopped onion
4 cups cooked pinto beans
3 cups canned tomatoes
1 small can tomato paste
1 cup chopped green pepper
½ cup chopped celery
½ cup sliced mushrooms
1 teaspoon Tabasco
2 Tablespoons fresh parsley, chopped
1 tablespoons cumin
1 tablespoon chili powder
2 teaspoons oregano
2 teaspoons garlic salt
2 teaspoons black pepper
1 teaspoon coriander

Brown ground beef with onions. Drain. Place in a large pot. Add remaining ingredients and bring to a boil. Reduce heat and simmer 1½ hours. Garnish with cheese and sour cream. This is delicious served in a bread boule (see index).

Soups

CORN CHOWDER

Serves 6-8

2 tablespoons butter
1 small onion, diced
3 cloves garlic, crushed
½ cup chopped celery
½ cup chopped carrots
1 cup chopped potatoes
3 cups chicken or vegetable broth
¼ cup butter
¼ cup flour
3 cups corn kernels
2 teaspoons thyme
1 tablespoon worcestershire sauce
2 cups half & half
salt and pepper to taste

In a large pot, sauté the onion and garlic in the 2 tablespoons butter until soft. Add the celery, carrots, potatoes and broth. Bring to a boil, then reduce heat and simmer until the vegetables are tender. Meanwhile, in a small saucepan, melt the ¼ cup of butter. Whisk in the flour and cook for 5 minutes, whisking. Add this roux to the soup when the vegetables are tender. Add all remaining ingredients, season to taste, and cook until thickened.

Breads and Muffins

Breads

HERB DINNER ROLLS

This is the most frequently requested recipe from the restaurant. A must-try! You can make larger rolls for sandwiches.

1 ounce dry yeast
2½ cups warm water
½ cup sugar
½ cup vegetable oil
½ cup finely diced onions
3 eggs
2 tablespoons molasses
2 tablespoons parsley
1 teaspoon anise seeds
1 teaspoon fennel seeds
1 teaspoon caraway seeds
½ tablespoon salt
1 cup cracked wheat
1 cup whole wheat flour
5-6 cups all-purpose flour

In a large bowl, combine the yeast and warm water. Let sit for 10 minutes. Add the next 12 ingredients and a few cups of the white flour, and mix well. Gradually add the remaining flour until the dough is no longer sticky. Knead the dough on a lightly floured surface, adding more flour as needed, until the dough is smooth and elastic. Place the dough in a greased bowl. Cover and set in a warm place to rise for 1 hour. Punch down dough and let rest for 10 minutes.

Form the dough into the desired size and shape. Place on a lightly greased baking sheet and let rise in a warm place for 45 minutes to an hour. Bake in a preheated 350 degree oven until lightly browned, about 15 to 20 minutes. Serve warm if possible.

Breads

SOURDOUGH STARTER

Every starter has a history, as they are passed between family and friends. Some can be 50 years old or more. My starter came from the Fullers in Sable, Idaho.

1 teaspoon yeast
1¼ cups warm water
1¼ cups flour
1 tablespoon sugar

Sourdough starter can be used in a variety of recipes, a few of which can be found in this book. Starter should be stored in the refrigerator, but bring it to room temperature when using it. If you can't use your starter for a week, feed it with ½ cup warm water and ½ cup flour, and leave it out overnight.

To make your starter, combine all ingredients in a non-metal bowl and mix with a wooden or plastic spoon. You can use white flour or whole wheat pastry flour. Lightly cover, and let sit at room temperature for 48 hours, or until it has a pleasant sour odor. Store in a glass or crockery jar covered with cheesecloth.

When you use 1 cup of starter in a recipe, stir in 1 cup of warm water and 1 cup of flour to replenish the starter. Let sit at room temperature for 12 hours.

Breads

SOURDOUGH BISCUITS

Makes 10-12 small biscuits

1½ cups flour
2 teaspoons baking powder
¼ teaspoon salt
⅓ cup butter
1 cup sourdough starter (see index)

Preheat oven to 375 degrees. In a non-metal bowl, mix flour, baking powder and salt. Cut in butter until mixture resembles coarse meal. Add starter and mix just until combined. Place dough on a lightly floured board and knead lightly. Pat or roll out to one inch thickness. Cut with a small round cutter and place biscuits on greased baking sheet. Bake 30 minutes, or until browned.

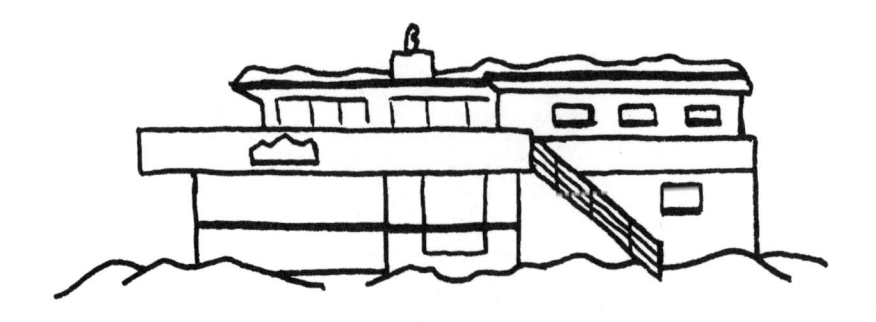

Breads

BANANA WALNUT MUFFINS

Yield: 18 muffins

3 eggs
1 cup sugar
½ cup vegetable oil
2 cups mashed bananas
1½ teaspoons baking soda
½ teaspoon salt
2½ cups flour
1 cup chopped walnuts

Preheat oven to 375 degrees. In a large bowl, combine eggs, sugar, oil and bananas. Mix well. In a separate bowl, mix remaining ingredients. Combine wet and dry mixtures and mix gently until just combined. Spoon into greased muffin pans. If desired, sprinkle additional walnuts on top of each muffin. Bake about 20 minutes, until browned. Remove from pan and cool on rack.

Breads

MEXICAN CORNBREAD

Serves 9-12

1¼ cups cornmeal
½ teaspoon baking soda
½ teaspoon salt
2 eggs
2 cups creamed corn
2 tablespoons diced jalapeños
½ cup diced green chiles
½ cup vegetable oil
¾ cup buttermilk
2 cups shredded cheddar cheese

Preheat oven to 375 degrees. Combine all ingredients. Mix by hand until well blended. Pour into greased 8" square pan. Bake until tester inserted in center comes out clean, about 25 minutes. Cut into squares and serve warm.

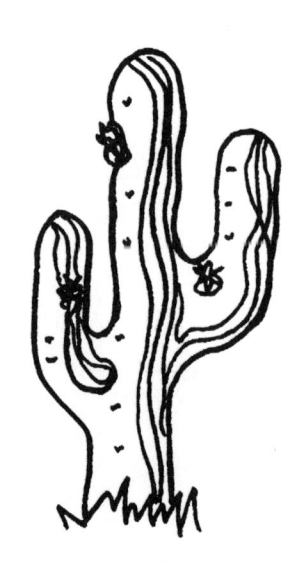

Breads

CORN CHEESE SCONES

Yield: 12 scones

1½ cups flour
½ cup cornmeal
2 tablespoons sugar
1½ teaspoons baking powder
⅛ teaspoon salt
6 tablespoons butter
½ cup shredded cheese
1 egg
½ cup milk

Preheat oven to 375 degrees. Combine first 5 ingredients in a mixing bowl. Cut in the butter until crumbly. Stir in cheese. In another bowl, whisk together the egg and milk. Combine wet and dry mixtures and mix just until it is all moistened.

Spread mixture into a 9-inch circle on a greased baking sheet. Score into desired size wedges. Bake 20 minutes or until lightly browned.

Slice along score marks and serve warm with butter.

The Slot was a natural rock slide clearing down the face of the Knob.

Breads

FRUIT SCONES

Be creative with your scones. For the fruit, try cranberries, dates, currants or blueberries. Our most popular combination is cranberry-date-pecan.

Yield: 12 scones

2 cups flour
¼ cup sugar
1½ teaspoons baking powder
⅛ teaspoon salt
6 tablespoons cold butter
1 egg
½ cup heavy cream
⅔ cup fruit and/or nuts

Preheat oven to 375 degrees. Combine flour, sugar, baking powder and salt in a mixing bowl. Cut in the butter until crumbly. In a separate bowl, whisk the egg and cream together, then add to the flour mixture. Stir just until combined. Stir in the fruit and/or nuts of your choice.

On a lightly greased baking sheet, spoon out the mixture, spreading it into a 9- inch circle. Score into 12 wedges. You may also use an ice cream scooper to scoop individual scones directly onto the baking sheet. Bake 20-25 minutes, or until browned.

Cut into wedges and serve with sweet butter and jam if desired.

Breads

FRENCH BREAD

2 packages active dry yeast
2½ cups warm water
1 tablespoon salt
approximately 8 cups all-purpose flour

Mix yeast and warm water (110 degrees) in a large bowl and let sit for 5 minutes. Add salt and 4 cups of the flour and mix well. Gradually add enough additional flour to make a soft dough. Knead on a lightly floured surface for about 10 minutes, adding additional flour as needed to make a smooth, elastic dough. Place in a greased bowl, cover and let rise in a warm place for 45 minutes, or until doubled. Punch down dough. Let rest for 10 minutes.

At this point, you are ready to shape the dough. Baguettes are long, thin loaves; you should get 3 to 4 loaves from this recipe. A boule is a round loaf which can be sliced, or hollowed out as a serving bowl for stew or chili. These are very popular at Dudley's. A boule should weigh 8 to 10 ounces. For bread sticks, simply roll pieces of dough into very thin ropes of the desired length, spray with water and sprinkle with sesame or poppy seeds.

Whatever shape you choose, place the shaped bread on a lightly greased cookie sheet and let rise in a warm place until doubled in size, about 1 hour. If desired, cut slits in the tops of the loaves with a serrated knife. Bake in a preheated 400 degree oven until golden brown. Baking time will vary with the size of the loaves. Remove the loaves from the pans to cool slightly before serving.

Breads

CINNAMON ROLLS

You have to be on the mountain early to get a cinnamon roll hot from the oven. They go fast!

Yield: 1 dozen rolls

¾ ounce dry yeast
⅓ cup warm water
¼ cup butter
1 cup milk
¼ cup sugar
2 eggs
1 teaspoon salt
4½ cups flour
3 tablespoons butter, melted
3 tablespoons sugar
1 tablespoon cinnamon
½ cup raisins (optional)

Icing:
4 tablespoons butter, softened
4 tablespoons cream cheese, softened
1½ cups powdered sugar
½ teaspoon vanilla
2 tablespoons milk

Combine yeast and warm water in a large bowl and set aside. Cut butter into small pieces, add to the milk, and heat until warm. Add the milk mixture to the yeast. Add the sugar, eggs, salt, and 3 cups of the flour, and beat mixture until smooth. Add the remaining flour, a small amount at a time, until the dough is no longer sticky. Knead 5 minutes on a lightly floured surface. Place the dough in a greased bowl. Cover and

Breads

set in a warm place to rise for 45 minutes. Punch down the dough and let rest for 5 minutes.

Roll out dough on a lightly floured surface to a 24x15 inch rectangle. Brush with the melted butter. Sprinkle with the sugar, cinnamon and raisins. Roll up from the long end and pinch edges to seal. Slice into 2 inch slices and place on a greased baking sheet. Let rise in a warm place for about an hour. Preheat oven to 350 degrees. Bake the rolls until lightly browned, about 12-15 minutes. Meanwhile, make the icing. Cream the butter and cream cheese together until light and fluffy. Add the remaining ingredients and beat well. Spread the icing on the cinnamon rolls while they are still warm, and serve immediately. These are the best!

Breads

FLOUR TORTILLAS

There's no comparison between homemade and store bought tortillas. Hot off the griddle, these are super!

Yield: 1 dozen tortillas

2 cups flour
1 teaspoon salt
1 teaspoon baking powder
¼ cup vegetable shortening
½ cup warm water

In a medium bowl, mix together the flour, salt, and baking powder. Cut in the vegetable shortening. Gradually add the water, until the mixture holds together. Knead lightly until smooth. Divide into 12 equal sized balls. Cover with plastic wrap and let rest for 30 minutes.

Heat a heavy skillet over medium-high heat. On a lightly floured surface, roll each ball into a thin circle, about 8 inches in diameter. Place the tortilla in the hot skillet and cook until lightly browned and speckled, about 1 to 2 minutes. Flip and cook the other side the same. If the tortillas puff up, just flatten them as they cook. Continue with the remaining dough balls until all are cooked, keeping them warm as you go. Serve warm.

Breads

BRAIDED EGG BREAD

Yield: 1 large loaf

1 package dry yeast
1 cup warm water (110 degrees)
¼ cup sugar
1 teaspoon salt
2 eggs
4 tablespoons butter or oil
3 to 4½ cups flour
1 egg
1 tablespoon water
3 tablespoons poppy or sesame seeds

Sprinkle yeast over the warm water in a large bowl. Add sugar. Let stand 5 minutes. Add salt, eggs, butter or oil, and 2 cups of flour. Beat until smooth. Continue adding flour, ¼ cup at a time, until the dough is stiff. Turn out onto a floured surface, and knead, adding more flour as needed, until the dough is smooth and elastic and no longer sticky. Place dough in a greased bowl. Cover and let rise in a warm place until doubled in size, about one hour. Punch down and let rest 10 minutes.

Turn out dough onto a lightly floured surface and divide into 3 equal portions. Roll each piece into an 18 inch long rope. Place the 3 ropes side by side, and braid. Gently lift the loaf onto a greased baking sheet. Pinch ends and tuck under. Let rise until doubled in size, about 45 minutes.

Preheat oven to 375 degrees. Mix the egg and water in a small bowl. Brush over the loaf. Sprinkle with the seeds. Bake until deep golden brown, about 45 minutes. Cool before slicing.

Breads

BLUEBERRY MUFFINS

Yield: 12-18 large muffins

2 eggs
1¼ cups milk
¾ cup vegetable oil
1¼ cups sugar
4 cups flour
1 tablespoon baking powder
½ teaspoon salt
2½ cups frozen or fresh blueberries

Preheat oven to 375 degrees. In a medium bowl, whisk eggs, milk, oil, and sugar. In a separate bowl, mix flour, baking powder, and salt. Combine wet and dry mixtures, and fold together gently until just mixed. Fold in blueberries. Spoon into greased muffin pans. Bake 20 to 30 minutes, until done. Let cool slightly in the pans, then remove and cool before serving.

Breads

BRAN MUFFINS

Yield: 12 muffins

Glaze (optional):
2 tablespoons butter, melted
¼ cup brown sugar
2 tablespoons honey
2 tablespoons corn syrup
1 tablespoon hot water

Muffins:
1 cup raisins
1¼ cups hot water
3 cups bran
1¼ cups flour
½ cup sugar
1½ teaspoons baking soda
½ teaspoon salt
½ cup vegetable oil
2 eggs
¾ cup buttermilk

To make the glaze, mix all ingredients in a microwave safe dish. Set aside. Soak raisins in hot water for at least 30 minutes. Add all remaining muffin ingredients to the raisin mixture, and mix well. Batter may be refrigerated at this point for up to a week, or used immediately.

Preheat oven to 350 degrees. Generously grease a 12-cup muffin pan. Microwave the glaze just until warm. Spoon 1 to 2 teaspoons of glaze into each cup. Fill with batter. Bake until done, about 20 minutes. Immediately flip pan upside down and remove muffins. Serve upside down, with the glaze on top.

Breads

PUMPKIN DATE MUFFINS

Yield: 12 muffins

2 eggs
1 cup pumpkin
½ cup vegetable oil
¾ cup sugar
2 cups flour
¼ teaspoon salt
1 teaspoon baking powder
¾ teaspoon baking soda
1 teaspoon cinnamon
1 cup chopped dates

Preheat oven to 375 degrees. In a medium bowl, whisk together first 4 ingredients. In a separate bowl, combine flour, salt, baking powder, baking soda, and cinnamon. Combine wet and dry ingredients and mix just until moistened. Stir in dates.

Spoon batter into greased muffin pans. Bake for 20 to 25 minutes, until done. Remove from pans and cool before serving.

> When a new employee gets a hold of Patti's recipes, you never know what's going to come out of the bakery, like the German chocolate carrot cake. But we don't mind - the employees get to eat the mistakes!
>
> -Mark 'Wally' Waldeck

Breads

PUMPKIN OATBRAN MUFFINS

Yield: 12 muffins

½ cup brown sugar
¼ cup orange juice
⅓ cup vegetable oil
½ cup canned pumpkin
2 egg whites
⅔ cup oatmeal
½ cup oatbran
1 cup flour
¼ teaspoon cinnamon
¼ teaspoon nutmeg
½ teaspoon vanilla
¼ teaspoon salt
2 teaspoons baking powder

Preheat oven to 375 degrees. Combine first 5 ingredients in a mixing bowl and stir well. Mix all remaining ingredients in a separate bowl, then add to the first mixture. Fold gently just until combined. Spoon into greased muffin pans. Sprinkle with oatmeal. Bake 25 to 30 minutes. Remove from pans to cool.

Breads

SOUR CREAM COFFEE CAKE

Topping:
⅔ cup brown sugar
1 cup chopped walnuts or pecans
2 tablespoons cinnamon

Cake:
⅓ pound butter
1 cup sugar
3 eggs
1 teaspoon vanilla
1 teaspoon baking soda
1½ teaspoons baking powder
2¼ cups flour
1½ cups sour cream

Preheat oven to 350 degrees. Combine all topping ingredients in a small bowl and set aside.

For the cake, cream the butter and sugar together. Add the eggs and vanilla and mix well. In a separate bowl, mix the dry ingredients together. Alternately add the dry ingredients and the sour cream to the butter mixture, beating after each addition.

Lightly grease a 9x13 inch baking pan. Spread half the batter into the pan. Sprinkle with half the topping. Spoon the remaining batter over, then sprinkle the remaining topping over that. Bake 35 minutes, or until the cake tests done in the middle. Sprinkle with powdered sugar when cool, if desired.

Breads

POTATO CARAWAY BREAD

1 package yeast
½ cup warm water
1 tablespoon sugar
2 cups warm potato water
1½ tablespoons salt
½ tablespoon caraway seeds
1 cup mashed potatoes
7½-8 cups flour

Combine yeast, ½ cup water and sugar. Let sit 20 minutes to proof. Add potato water, salt, caraway seeds, potatoes, and 4 cups flour. Beat well. Gradually add remaining flour, until dough is no longer sticky. Knead on a lightly floured surface for 10 minutes. Place in a greased bowl, covered, in a warm place, for 1 hour. Punch down, let rest 5 minutes. Form into one large round loaf, or rolls, or 2 regular loaves. Set in a warm place to rise 1 hour more. Preheat oven to 400 degrees. Bake until browned. Time will vary depending on the size of the loaves.

Breads

FRUIT, NUT & VEGETABLE BREAD

Yield: 1 loaf

2 eggs
½ cup vegetable oil
¾ cup sugar
1 teaspoon vanilla
½ cup flour
1 cup whole wheat flour
¾ teaspoon baking soda
½ teaspoon salt
1½ teaspoons cinnamon
1 cup shredded raw zucchini
½ cup shredded coconut
1 cup chopped pecans
1 cup chopped dates
1 cup raisins

Preheat the oven to 350 degrees. Beat together the first 4 ingredients. Add the next 5 ingredients and mix well. Stir in all remaining ingredients. Pour the batter into a greased 9x5-inch loaf pan. Bake for about 1 hour, or until the loaf tests done. Cool for 10 minutes before removing from the pan.

Dressings, Sauces and Condiments

Dressings

AVOCADO RELISH

Serve this relish with just about any Mexican dish, or with a basket of tortilla chips for dipping.

Yield: about 1 cup

1 firm avocado, diced
1 tomato, seeded and diced
½ red onion, diced
2 tablespoons cider vinegar
2 tablespoons olive oil
1 clove garlic, chopped
1 teaspoon fresh cilantro, chopped
salt & pepper to taste

Combine all ingredients in a bowl and toss lightly until combined. Chill for about an hour to allow the flavors to mingle. Best served the same day it is made.

Dressings

MEXICAN SALSA

Yield: 3 cups

2 cups diced tomatoes, fresh or canned
½ cup diced green chiles
3 tablespoons diced jalapeños
¼ cup diced onion
1 tablespoon chopped fresh cilantro
salt & pepper to taste

Combine first 5 ingredients in a bowl and mix gently. Season to taste with salt and pepper. Add more jalapeños if you like a hotter salsa.

Dressings

TOMATILLO SAUCE

This sauce is especially good on Dudley's huevos or chicken enchiladas (see index).

1 tablespoon butter or oil
2 cloves garlic, chopped
1 small onion, diced
1 lb. fresh tomatillos (or 32 oz. canned)
1 cup diced green chiles
¼ teaspoon black pepper
¼ teaspoon ground coriander
¼ teaspoon salt
1 cup chicken broth
2 tablespoons cornstarch

Sauté garlic and onion in the butter or oil until soft. If using fresh tomatillos, remove husks and pureé in blender until smooth. If using canned tomatillos, drain and pureé. Add the tomatillos to the onions in the pot. Add the remaining ingredients and cook until thickened. Adjust seasonings to your own taste.

Ute Chute was named for its chute-like effect and the former Indian inhabitants of the area.

Dressings

SUNDRIED TOMATO VINAIGRETTE

Yield: ¾ cup

¼ cup sundried tomatoes
1 tablespoon Dijon mustard
1 tablespoon honey
¼ cup red wine vinegar
¼ cup olive oil
salt & pepper to taste

Reconstitute the sundried tomatoes in hot water for about 10 minutes. Drain.

Place the tomatoes and all remaining ingredients in a food processor and process until thick and smooth. Adjust seasonings.

Dressings

RASPBERRY VINAIGRETTE

Yield: 2 cups

1 cup vegetable oil
1 cup raspberry vinegar
2 tablespoons Dijon mustard
1 tablespoons sugar
¼ cup frozen raspberries, thawed

Combine all ingredients in a food processor and process for 1 minute.

POPPY SEED DRESSING

Yield: 2 cups

1½ cups vegetable oil
½ cup red wine vinegar
3 tablespoons minced white onion
1 teaspoon salt
2 tablespoons poppy seeds
1 teaspoon dry mustard
½ cup sugar

Combine all ingredients in a food processor and process until the mixture thickens, up to five minutes.

Dressings

KIWI-LIME VINAIGRETTE

Yield: 1 cup

1 kiwi fruit
juice of 4 limes
4 tablespoons cider vinegar
⅓ cup walnut oil
2 tablespoons fresh mint, chopped
2 teaspoons honey
1 tablespoon cumin

Peel the kiwi fruit and place in a food processor with the remaining ingredients and process until smooth.

HONEY MUSTARD DRESSING

Yield: 2 cups

¼ cup cider vinegar
3 tablespoons honey
½ cup mayonnaise
¼ cup Dijon mustard
2 tablespoons diced onion
2 tablespoons fresh parsley
¾ cup vegetable oil

Combine all ingredients in a food processor and process until smooth.

Dressings

ENCHILADA SAUCE

Yield: 4½ cups

1¼ cups tomato pureé (canned)
2½ cups water
2 cloves garlic, minced
½ cup diced green chiles
⅓ cup diced onions
⅓ cup red chile pureé (if unavailable, use pure red chile powder, found in the Mexican section of the grocery store)
1 teaspoon black pepper
1 teaspoon oregano
1 teaspoon coriander
3 tablespoons cornstarch, dissolved in small amount cold water
1 chicken bouillon cube

Put everything in a saucepan and simmer for 20 minutes.

Dressings

CARROT-SESAME DRESSING

To use this delicious dressing as a dip, omit the water until last, then add just enough for the desired consistency.

Yield: 2 cups

1 cup cooked carrots
¾ cup rice wine vinegar
½ cup water
¼ cup olive oil
1 teaspoon garlic, crushed
2 tablespoons apple juice concentrate
2 tablespoons Tamari
1 teaspoon ginger powder
2 tablespoons toasted sesame seeds

Combine all ingredients in a food processor and blend until smooth. Refrigerate overnight.

Dressings

CHUTNEY VINAIGRETTE

This versatile dressing is delicious on pasta salads as well as green salads. Or try it as a marinade for chicken.

Yield: 1½ cups

½ cup olive oil
½ cup red wine vinegar
¼ cup prepared chutney
¼ cup plain yogurt
2 tablespoons smooth peanut butter

Process all ingredients in a food processor until smooth.

Salads and Side Dishes

Salads and Sides

MIXED BEAN SALAD

Serves 6-8

6 ounces dried beans, mixed varieties
2 tablespoons olive oil
2 tablespoons balsamic vinegar
1 teaspoon sugar
1 cup frozen or fresh corn kernels
¼ cup diced red onion
½ cup diced green peppers
½ cup diced red peppers
½ cup prepared salsa
2 tablespoons chopped cilantro
salt to taste

Soak beans overnight. Drain and rinse. Place the beans in a pot with fresh water and bring to a boil. Cook until tender, but not mushy. Drain and chill.

Combine beans with all remaining ingredients and mix gently. Chill several hours or overnight.

We had over 300 inches of snow during the 92-93 ski season. I know, because it was my job to clear it off the decks at Dudley's. Waking up to a foot or two of powder meant one thing to me - a lot of work!

-Brian Morris

Salads and Sides

LOWFAT COLESLAW

Serves 4-6

2 cups shredded green cabbage
½ cup shredded red cabbage
½ cup shredded carrots
½ cup plain yogurt
2 tablespoons buttermilk
1 tablespoon mayonnaise
1 tablespoon cider vinegar
½ tablespoon sugar
½ tablespoon Dijon mustard
¼ teaspoon celery salt
dash of cayenne pepper

Mix all ingredients in a large bowl. Adjust seasonings to taste. Chill well before serving.

Salads and Sides

CAESAR SALAD

Serves 6-8

⅔ cup olive oil
¼ cup red wine vinegar
2 tablespoons fresh lemon juice
6 anchovy filets, minced
3 cloves garlic, diced
1 tablespoon Dijon mustard
1 teaspoon white pepper
1 cup freshly grated parmesan cheese
1 large head romaine lettuce
croutons

Blend first 7 ingredients in a food processor. Add ½ cup of the parmesan cheese and blend again.

Wash the romaine lettuce and tear into bite-sized pieces. Place in a large bowl, pour the dressing over and toss to coat. Dish onto serving plates and sprinkle with remaining cheese and croutons.

Zugspitz was named and dedicated after the mountain in Europe, when Aspen and Garmish became sister cities in the 1960's and trail names were exchanged between the two cities.

Salads and Sides

PESTO POTATO SALAD

Serves 4-6

4 cups cooked, chopped potatoes
2 hard-cooked eggs, diced (optional)
¼ cup diced red onion
½ cup diced celery
1 tablespoon Dijon mustard
2 tablespoons mayonnaise
¼ cup plain yogurt
¼ cup prepared pesto sauce
salt & pepper to taste

Combine all ingredients in a large bowl. Toss lightly. Season to taste. Garnish with red pepper rings.

Salads and Sides

ORIENTAL NOODLE SALAD

Serves 6-8

Dressing:
⅓ cup red wine vinegar
⅓ cup apple juice concentrate
1 tablespoon orange juice concentrate
2 tablespoons sesame oil
2 tablespoons soy sauce
2 tablespoons water
1 tablespoon peanut butter
1 teaspoon grated fresh ginger
½ teaspoon chile paste

Salad:
8 ounces cooked vermicelli
2 cups cooked, shredded chicken
½ cup chopped green onions
2 cups shredded green cabbage
½ cup sliced celery
½ cup thinly sliced red pepper
½ cup sliced water chestnuts
¼ lb. snow peas, steamed

In a small bowl, combine all dressing ingredients and whisk until thoroughly mixed. Set aside.

In a large bowl, place all salad ingredients. Pour dressing over and toss lightly. Chill before serving.

Follow your own preferences for building your salad. For instance, if you don't like cabbage, substitute lettuce, or if you're a vegetarian, just omit the chicken.

Salads and Sides

MARINATED SHRIMP & VEGETABLE SALAD

Serves 6-8

1 lb. medium to large shrimp, cooked, peeled & deveined
1 cup mushrooms, quartered
1 cup artichoke hearts, quartered
1 cup sliced green onions
1 large red pepper, cut into 1 inch chunks
1 cup broccoli florets, lightly steamed
1 cup cauliflower florets, lightly steamed
2 tablespoons olive oil
2 tablespoons balsamic vinegar
1 tablespoon lemon juice
1 teaspoon dijon mustard
1 clove garlic, crushed
½ teaspoons salt
¼ teaspoon black pepper
lettuce
fresh parsley

In a large bowl, place the shrimp and all of the vegetables. Set aside. In a separate bowl, whisk together the next 7 ingredients. Pour the dressing over the vegetables and toss to coat. Cover bowl and refrigerate at least several hours.

Serve on individual beds of lettuce, with diced fresh parsley sprinkled over the top.

Salads and Sides

POTATOES AND CARROTS IN CREAM

Serves 4-6

3 large carrots
3 large russet potatoes
(You should have enough vegetables to measure 5 ½ cups)
1 ¼ cups milk
½ cup heavy cream
salt & pepper to taste
⅛ teaspoon nutmeg
¼ cup freshly grated parmesan cheese
1 tablespoon diced fresh parsley

Cut carrots into ⅛ inch rounds. Peel potatoes and cut into thin slices, about 1/16 inch. This is most easily done in a food processor.

Bring the milk, cream, salt, pepper and nutmeg to a boil in a skillet. Add the potatoes and carrots. Stir. Let simmer, stirring often, until done, about 25 minutes.

Preheat broiler just before the potatoes are finished cooking. Turn the potato mixture into a baking dish. Sprinkle with the cheese and broil until nicely browned. Sprinkle with parsley and serve immediately.

Salads and Sides

TWICE BAKED POTATOES

Serves 4-8

4 large baking potatoes
4 tablespoons milk
4 tablespoons sour cream
2 tablespoons butter, softened
4 ounces cheddar cheese, grated
4 slices bacon, cooked and crumbled
2 green onions, diced
salt and pepper to taste
dash paprika

Preheat oven to 400 degrees. Pierce the potatoes, place in the oven and bake until tender, about 1¼ hours. Remove and let stand 5 minutes.

Cut each potato in half lengthwise, and using a spoon, scoop out pulp, leaving ¼-inch thick shells. Set the shells aside.

Place the potato pulp in a bowl. Add the milk, sour cream, butter, and half of the cheese. Mash well. Stir in the bacon and onions, and season to taste with salt and pepper. Spoon this mixture into the potato shells, and place on a baking sheet. Sprinkle with the remaining cheese and paprika. Return to the oven until heated through, about 10 minutes.

Salads and Sides

MEXICAN RICE

Serves 8

¼ cup chopped onion
1 tablespoon butter or olive oil
2 cups rice (uncooked)
3 cups water
1 cup enchilada sauce (see index, or use canned)
1 tablespoon garlic salt
1½ tablespoons chile powder
½ teaspoon black pepper

Sauté onion in butter or oil until tender. Add remaining ingredients. Bring to a boil, then reduce heat to simmer. Cover and continue cooking until all liquid is absorbed, approximately 20 minutes.

Salads and Sides

ROASTED ROSEMARY POTATOES

Serves 4-6

4 baking potatoes
2 tablespoons olive oil
2 tablespoons fresh rosemary
coarse kosher salt
pepper

Preheat oven to 400 degrees. Quarter the potatoes and place in a mixing bowl. Drizzle with the olive oil, and toss to coat evenly. Place on a baking sheet. Sprinkle with the rosemary, salt and pepper. Bake until tender, about 20-30 minutes.

Variation: omit the rosemary and sprinkle with chili powder.

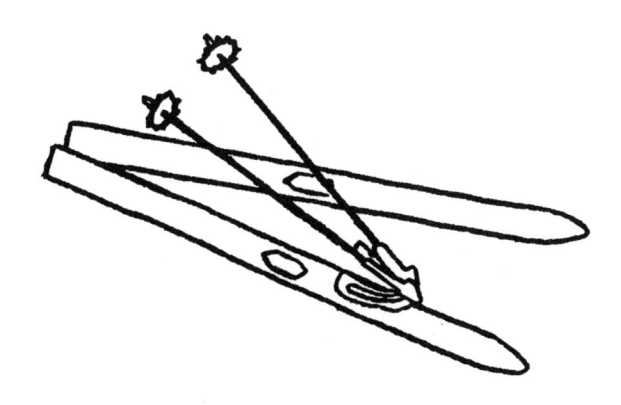

Salads and Sides

FRUITY SWEET POTATO PUREE

Serves 4

4 cups chopped sweet potatoes or yams
1 banana or 1 peach, peeled
2 tablespoons butter
1 tablespoon bourbon
1 teaspoon brown sugar
1 tablespoon butter
½ cup sliced almonds

Place sweet potatoes in a pot, cover with water and boil until tender. Drain. Place potatoes, banana, butter, bourbon and sugar in a food processor, and process until smooth, scraping down the sides of the workbowl once or twice. Melt the 1 tablespoon butter in a small pan, add the almonds and cook, stirring, until the almonds are golden. Serve the puree hot, garnished with the almonds.

Salads and Sides

VEGETABLE RICE PILAF

Serves 4-6

1 tablespoon butter
½ onion, diced
2 cloves garlic, crushed
1 carrot, diced
2 ribs of celery, diced
1 cup sliced mushrooms
1 cup white rice, uncooked
2½ cups vegetable or chicken broth
1 tablespoon soy sauce
1 teaspoon sesame oil
1 tablespoon fresh dill

Melt butter in medium sauce pan. Add onions and sauté until tender. Add garlic, carrots, celery and mushrooms and sauté 3 minutes. Add remaining ingredients. Bring to boil and continue to boil until water level goes down to the rice level. Reduce heat to low, cover and simmer about 10 minutes, or until water has all been absorbed.

You can't find a better place than Dudley's for the scenery, skiing, hospitality, and cuisine. We love it so much we were married there during a snowstorm in 1993.

-Pat & Rae Ann Hunter

Salads and Sides

PARMESAN POTATO STICKS

Serves 4-6

¼ cup bread crumbs
½ cup parmesan cheese
¼ teaspoon basil
¼ teaspoon thyme
¼ teaspoon oregano
¼ teaspoon salt
⅛ teaspoon pepper
4 cups potato sticks (½" by ½")
2 tablespoons vegetable oil

Preheat the oven to 400 degrees. Place the bread crumbs, cheese and spices in a shallow dish. Place the oil in another dish. Dip each potato into the oil, scraping off any excess, then roll in the crumbs and place on a lightly greased baking sheet. Bake for 20 minutes, or until the potatoes are tender.

Salads and Sides

ZUCCHINI POTATO PANCAKES

Serves 4

1 medium zucchini, grated (about 1 cup)
2 medium potatoes, grated (about 2 cups)
½ onion, chopped
2 eggs
2 tablespoons flour
½ teaspoon salt
⅛ teaspoon pepper
1 tablespoon butter or oil
sour cream
applesauce

Place the grated zucchini, potatoes and the chopped onion in a food processor fitted with a steel blade. Pulse on and off several times to thoroughly and finely chop the vegetables, but don't puree. Place mixture in a bowl and add the eggs, flour, salt and pepper. In a non-stick skillet, melt about 1 teaspoon of butter. Drop about ¼ cup of potato mixture for each pancake, pressing down with a spoon to form a pancake. Brown on both sides, approximately 3-4 minutes per side. Keep warm and repeat with remaining batter, adding more butter or oil as needed. Serve hot with sour cream and applesauce.

Salads and Sides

MARINATED GREENS

Serves 4-6

Lemon Caper Dressing:
½ cup olive oil
½ cup lemon juice
¼ cup tarragon vinegar
2 tablespoons Dijon mustard
1 teaspoon sugar
3 tablespoons capers

1 tablespoon olive oil
1 small red onion
6 cups mixed greens and lettuces
½ cup julienned red peppers
½ cup julienned yellow peppers
¼ cup toasted pine nuts

Prepare the dressing. Place all ingredients in a bowl and whisk thoroughly. Set aside.

In a small pan, heat the olive oil. Cut the onion into quarters, then slice. Sauté in the oil until soft. Cool. In a salad bowl, place the greens, lettuce, peppers and sautéed onions. Pour enough dressing over to coat and toss lightly. Sprinkle the pine nuts over and serve.

Entrees

Entrees

CHEESE OR CHICKEN ENCHILADAS

Serves 6

12 corn tortillas
1 cup vegetable oil
1½ lbs. grated cheddar or jack cheese
¾ cup finely diced onions
3 cups shredded cooked chicken (optional)
1 recipe enchilada sauce (see index)
sour cream
guacamole
black olives

Prepare enchilada sauce. Keep warm while preparing the enchiladas.

Preheat the oven to 350 degrees. Heat the oil in a skillet to about 400 degrees. Fry each tortilla a few seconds on each side to soften. Dip each tortilla into the warm sauce, then place on a plate. Fill with cheese and a small amount of onion, and chicken if desired. Roll up and place seam side down in a baking pan. Repeat with the remaining tortillas. Pour remaining sauce over the top of the enchiladas, making sure they are all smothered. Sprinkle the top with any remaining cheese. Cover with foil and bake until heated through, about 20 to 30 minutes. Garnish with sour cream, guacamole or olives.

Entrees

TAMALE PIE

Serves 6-8

15-20 dried corn husks
2 cups frozen corn kernels, thawed
1 cup Masa Harina
1 16 oz. can creamed corn
1¼ teaspoons baking powder
1 egg
½ cup melted butter
½ cup hot chicken broth
5 Anaheim or Poblano chiles, roasted, peeled and chopped (or 2 4oz. cans green chiles)
2 cups cooked chicken meat, shredded
1 cup shredded jack or cheddar cheese
Mexican salsa (see index)

Soak corn husks in hot water for several hours. Grease a 10 inch pie pan and line with the husks, with the pointed ends extending over the sides of the pan. Set aside.

Place the corn in a food processor and process for 30 seconds. Add the Masa Harina, the creamed corn, the egg and the baking powder and process until blended. While the machine is running, add the melted butter and the chicken broth.

Pour ⅔ of the batter over the corn husks. Sprinkle the chiles, chicken and cheese over the batter. Top with the remaining batter.

Loosely cover the pan with aluminum foil, being careful not to let the foil touch the topping. Bake for 1½ hours, or until set. Remove foil and let sit for 5 minutes. Cut into wedges and serve with Mexican salsa.

Entrees

NAVAJO TACOS

The fry bread can also be made as a dessert. Just sprinkle with powdered sugar or serve drizzled with honey.

Serves 8

Fry Bread:
2 cups flour
1 tablespoon baking powder
½ teaspoon salt
2 tablespoons shortening
¾ cup hot water
oil for frying

Fillings:
3 cups heated refried beans
shredded lettuce
diced tomatoes
grated cheddar cheese
sour cream
salsa
double recipe of avocado relish (see index)

To make the fry bread, combine flour, baking powder and salt in a mixing bowl. Cut in the shortening. Stir in water with a fork. Knead until smooth. Let rest for 5 minutes. Divide into 8 pieces. Roll each piece into an 8 inch circle. Poke a hole in the center of each. Fry in 2 inches of hot oil (375 degrees) until golden brown. Turn and brown other side. Drain on paper towels.

Top each piece of fry bread with refried beans and your choice of other toppings.

Entrees

CHICKEN QUESADILLAS

These are our most popular quesadillas, although we offer beef and vegetable fillings as well. Be creative and use whatever filling appeals to you.

Serves 6

3 cups shredded cooked chicken meat
½ cup diced green chiles (fresh or canned)
¼ cup sliced black olives
1 tablespoon chili powder
1 teaspoon black pepper
1 teaspoon garlic salt
½ cup sour cream
6 flour tortillas
1 pound grated cheddar or jack cheese

Mix first 7 ingredients together. Adjust seasonings to taste. Heat a large skillet. Brush tortillas on one side with oil or butter, and lay oiled side down in the warm skillet. Sprinkle with cheese, then spoon some chicken filling over half of the tortilla. When the cheese starts to melt, fold over in half. Cook until filling is warm, browning both sides. Continue with remaining tortillas as space allows. You can keep the quesadillas warm in the oven until they're all browned. Garnish with shredded lettuce, chopped tomatoes, salsa, or our tomatillo sauce (see index).

Entrees

GRILLED SALMON WITH ROASTED RED PEPPER SAUCE

Serves 4

3 large red peppers
1 teaspoon olive oil
4 cloves garlic, crushed
¼ cup white wine
2 teaspoons balsamic vinegar
1 tablespoon fresh basil, chopped
salt and pepper to taste
4 salmon fillets

Preheat grill or broiler. Broil the peppers until charred on all sides. Let sit until cool enough to handle. Remove skins, stem and seeds. Place in a food processor or blender and pureé. Place in a small bowl. In a small saucepan, sauté garlic in olive oil until soft. Add the wine, bring to a boil and reduce to ½. Add to the pepper pureé. Add vinegar, basil, salt and pepper to taste.

Grill the salmon until done, approximately 3-4 minutes per side. Serve with the pepper sauce spooned over the top.

Dudley's was not just an excellent place to work, but it was the place to meet. On your ski days, you could just stop by anytime and find someone to hang out with. It was like your family away from home.

-Joanne Burke

Entrees

CHILAQUILES

Serves 6

Vegetable oil for frying
18 corn tortillas
3 cups enchilada sauce, red or green (see index)
4 cups cooked shredded chicken meat
3 cups shredded jack or cheddar cheese
1 cup sour cream
garnishes

Heat ½ inch of oil in a small skillet. Cut tortillas into 8 wedges each, and fry in batches until half-crisp. Drain on paper towels.

Preheat oven to 350 degrees. Grease 6 individual casserole dishes or a 2 quart dish. To assemble, place half the chips in the casserole, sprinkle half the chicken meat over, then dab on a bit of sour cream. Pour half the sauce over, then half the cheese. Repeat all the layers, ending with the cheese. Bake until heated through and the cheese melts, 15-20 minutes, depending on the size dishes you are using. Garnish with your choice of olives, lettuce, tomatoes, guacamole, or any combination.

This is delicious with a fried egg on top, served anytime of day.

Entrees

CHICKEN POT PIE

6 Servings

Crust:
1½ cups flour
½ teaspoon salt
½ cup cold butter
⅓ cup ice water
2 tablespoons milk

Filling:
4 carrots, diced
2 tablespoons butter
1 large onion, diced
4 stalks celery, sliced
4 tablespoon flour
2 cups rich chicken broth
1 cup cream
¼ cup white wine
1 tablespoon Dijon mustard
1 tablespoon tarragon
1 tablespoon fresh parsley
salt and pepper to taste
1 cup peas
2 cups cooked diced chicken meat

To make the crust, mix flour and salt in a bowl, then cut in the butter until it resembles coarse meal. Sprinkle with the water and mix until it forms a dough. Knead lightly until it all sticks together. Wrap in plastic and refrigerate.
Cook carrots in a small amount of water until tender. Set

Entrees

aside. In a large pot, melt the butter. Add onion and cook until almost tender. Add celery and continue cooking about 5 minutes. Sprinkle the flour over the onion-celery mixture, and cook, stirring for 3-4 minutes. Slowly add the broth, cream and wine, and whisk until smooth, cooking until it thickens. Add mustard and spices, then stir in peas, carrots and chicken. Adjust seasonings. Remove from heat and pour into a 2 quart casserole dish.

Preheat oven to 425 degrees. Roll out the dough on a lightly floured board to fit the shape and size of the casserole dish. Place the dough over the filling. Pierce with a fork in several places and crimp the edges. Brush with the 2 tablespoons milk.

Place the dish on a baking sheet in the oven and bake for 20-30 minutes, until the crust is browned.

Entrees

TROPICAL GRILLED FISH

Serves 4

Salsa:
¼ cup finely diced red onion
2 teaspoons grated ginger
½ teaspoon curry powder
1 large papaya, finely chopped
2 tablespoons fresh lime juice
1 tablespoon finely chopped cilantro

Marinade:
2 tablespoons olive oil
2 tablespoons fresh lime juice
1 tablespoon finely chopped cilantro

4 fish steaks (Ahi, Marlin or Swordfish)

Place all salsa ingredients in a small bowl and mix lightly. Refrigerate several hours or overnight. Whisk marinade ingredients together and pour over the fish in a shallow pan. Refrigerate 2-3 hours.

Preheat grill or broiler. Grill fish until done, about 4 minutes per side. Time will vary depending on thickness of fish and temperature of grill. Serve with papaya salsa and lime wedges.

Entrees

SMOKED TROUT FETTUCCINE

Serves 4-6

⅔ lb. fettuccine
2 cups heavy cream
1 tablespoon diced shallots
1 tomato
½ lb. sugar snap peas
5 oz. smoked trout, flaked
¼ cup grated parmesan cheese
salt and pepper

Cook the fettuccine according to package directions. While the pasta is cooking, place the cream and shallots in a large pot, bring to a boil and continue boiling about 3 minutes. Seed and dice the tomato, chop the peas, and add both to the cream. Add the trout. Continue to boil 2 more minutes. When the pasta is cooked, drain and place in a large bowl. Add the parmesan cheese to the cream mixture, season to taste with salt and pepper, then pour over the pasta. Toss lightly to coat the pasta, and serve immediately.

Entrees

FRIED SCALLOPS & GREENS

Serves 4

2 tablespoons peanut oil
1 lb. scallops
4 green onions, diced
2 cloves garlic, minced
½ teaspoon fresh ginger, minced
½ lb. fresh spinach or Swiss chard, chopped
2 teaspoons cornstarch
1 teaspoon sesame oil
1 teaspoon soy sauce
⅔ cup rich chicken broth
salt and pepper to taste
3 cups cooked white rice

Heat a wok or large skillet. Add 1 tablespoon peanut oil, then the scallops. Quickly stir-fry just until cooked through. Remove scallops, add a little more oil if needed, then add the onions, garlic and ginger and stir-fry 30 seconds. Add the greens and cook until limp. In a small bowl, mix the remaining ingredients and add to the wok. Cook just until thickened, then add the scallops and toss. Serve hot on a bed of plain white rice

Entrees

SOUTHWESTERN CHICKEN KIEV

Serves 4

4 boneless skinless chicken breasts
4 Anaheim chiles, roasted, peeled and seeded
3 ounces goat cheese
salt and pepper
¼ cup bread crumbs
¼ cup cornmeal
2 teaspoons chile powder
1 teaspoon cumin
½ teaspoon garlic salt
6 tablespoons melted butter
Salsa (see index)

Preheat oven to 375 degrees. Pound chicken breasts between 2 sheets of wax paper until thin. Place one chile and ¼ of the goat cheese on each breast. Season with salt and pepper. Roll up and secure with a toothpick.

In a shallow dish, combine bread crumbs, cornmeal, and spices. Roll each breast in the melted butter, then in the crumb mixture.

Place on a baking sheet and bake for 30 minutes. Remove toothpicks. Serve with salsa.

Entrees

VEGETABLE LASAGNA

Serves 6

Tomato Cream Sauce:
1 teaspoon olive oil
½ onion, diced
1 clove garlic, crushed
2 cups tomato sauce
1 tablespoon fresh basil
½ cup milk
1 teaspoon cornstarch
salt and pepper

1 tablespoon butter
½ onion, diced
1 clove garlic, crushed
½ cup diced red peppers
½ cup diced zucchini
1 cup sliced mushrooms
2 cups chopped fresh spinach
1 cup chopped broccoli, steamed
1 cup ricotta cheese
4 oz. goat cheese (optional)
1 egg
¼ cup grated Parmesan cheese
salt and pepper
1½ cups shredded mozzarella
6 oz. lasagna noodles, cooked al dente

Entrees

Prepare the tomato cream sauce. In a medium saucepan, sauté onion and garlic in oil for about 5 minutes. Add remaining ingredients and bring to a boil. Reduce heat and simmer, stirring constantly until thickened. Set aside.

For filling, sauté onion and garlic in butter. Add peppers, zucchini and mushrooms and sauté until vegetables are almost tender. Add spinach and cook until wilted. In a medium bowl, place sautéd vegetables, broccoli, ricotta cheese, goat cheese, egg and Parmesan cheese. Season with salt and pepper.

Preheat oven to 350 degrees. In a 9x9- inch baking dish, spread a thin layer of sauce. Layer ⅓ of the noodles, then ½ of the vegetable mixture. Sprinkle with a little mozzarella and spoon on a layer of sauce. Repeat. End with noodles, sauce and mozzarella. Bake at 350 degrees for 30-40 minutes, until hot in the middle.

Entrees

TORTELLINI WITH PROSCIUTTO CREAM SAUCE

Serves 4-6

1½ lbs. fresh cheese tortellini
1 tablespoon butter
¼ cup minced green onions
½ lb. prosciutto, cut into thin strips
1½ cups heavy cream
¾ cup freshly grated Parmesan cheese
salt and pepper

Cook the tortellini al dente. Drain. Set aside in large bowl. In a large skillet, melt butter. Add green onions and cook 3 minutes. Add prosciutto and cream. Bring to a boil, reduce heat and simmer 8-10 minutes. Add ½ cup Parmesan cheese. Season to taste with salt and pepper. Pour over tortellini and toss lightly to coat. Serve immediately, with additional Parmesan cheese sprinkled over the top.

Entrees

SPANAKOPITA

Yield: 9" square pan or 6-9 servings

1 package Filo pastry, thawed
4 tablespoons butter
6 tablespoons olive oil
¾ cup chopped onion
1 lb. fresh spinach, cleaned and chopped
8 oz. cream cheese
8 oz. feta cheese
1 teaspoon black pepper
2 eggs

Preheat oven to 375 degrees. Melt 4 tablespoons butter and add 4 tablespoons olive oil. Set aside. In a heavy skillet, sauté the onions in the remaining olive oil until soft. Add the spinach and cook until wilted. Add the cream cheese and stir until soft. Remove from heat. Crumble the feta cheese into the spinach mixture, then add the pepper and eggs and stir until well combined.

Remove the Filo pastry from its wrapper, and cut out a section the size of the pan; rewrap the remainder for another use. Layer 10 sheets of pastry in the pan, brushing each layer with the butter-olive oil mixture. Spread the spinach filling over the pastry. Repeat the layering and brushing with the butter mixture for 10 more layers. Using a serrated knife, cut through the top pastry layers to make 6 or 9 squares, depending on the size servings you want. Bake for 1 hour, or until golden brown.

Entrees

PASTA PRIMAVERA WITH ASIAGO

Serves 6

1 lb. pasta, any shape
2 carrots, julienned
1 cup asparagus, sliced into 1 inch slices
1 cup broccoli florets
3 tablespoons olive oil
2 cloves garlic, minced
1 medium zucchini, sliced
2 tablespoons fresh basil
¾ cup grated asiago cheese
salt and pepper to taste

Cook the pasta al dente. Place in a large bowl. Set aside. Steam the carrots, broccoli and asparagus until just tender. Set aside. In a skillet, sauté the garlic in the olive oil for 1 minute. Add the zucchini and cook until just tender. Add the basil and the other steamed vegetables and heat through. Add this mixture to the pasta, add the cheese and toss gently. Serve immediately.

You may substitute romano or parmesan cheese for the asiago. Use only freshly grated cheese.

Entrees

HERB-BROILED ORANGE ROUGHY

Serves 4

2 pounds orange roughy fillets
2 tablespoons mayonaisse
2 tomatoes, seeded and chopped
⅓ cup diced green onions
2 tablespoons lemon juice
2 tablespoons chopped fresh parsley
1 tablespoon chopped fresh basil
1 tablespoon chopped fresh oregano
1 tablespoon garlic, crushed
2 teaspoons Dijon style mustard
salt and pepper

Preheat the broiler. Place the fish fillets in a lightly greased baking pan. In a small bowl, combine all remaining ingredients and spread over the fish. Broil 8-10 minutes, until the fish is cooked through. Garnish with lemon wedges and sprigs of fresh herbs.

Entrees

SOLE FLORENTINE

Serves 4

2 tablespoons butter
2 tablespoons flour
1 cup milk
1 teaspoon chicken bouillon
dash nutmeg
dash Tabasco
½ cup shredded Swiss cheese
salt and pepper to taste
12 oz. fresh spinach, washed and stemmed
1½ pounds sole fillets
1 tablespoon fresh lemon juice
2 tablespoons parmesan cheese
dash paprika

Preheat oven to 350 degrees. In a small pan, melt the butter. Add flour and cook, whisking constantly for 3 minutes. Slowly add milk, whisking until smooth. Add bouillon, nutmeg, Tabasco, salt and pepper to taste and cook on low heat until thickened. Stir in Swiss cheese. Set aside.

In a 9x13-inch baking pan, place spinach leaves. Arrange fish over the spinach and sprinkle with lemon juice. Pour sauce over. Sprinkle with parmesan cheese and paprika. Bake for 20 minutes, or until fish is done.

Entrees

SESAME CHICKEN

Serves 4-6

⅓ cup soy sauce
¼ cup white wine
¼ cup brown sugar
¼ cup oil
¼ cup toasted sesame seeds
½ teaspoon grated ginger
1 teaspoon chili powder
1 small onion, diced
2 cloves garlic, crushed
4-6 boneless chicken breasts, or 3 lb. cup up chicken

Put all ingredients in a medium bowl and mix. Marinate chicken overnight. Broil, barbecue or bake until cooked through, basting frequently with the marinade.

Entrees

GRILLED AHI WITH TOMATILLO-APPLE RELISH

Serves 6

6 Ahi steaks (or fish of your choice)
1 cup teriyaki sauce
¼ lb. fresh tomatillos
½ Granny Smith apple, peeled
3 tablespoons chopped red onion
1 lime
1 tablespoon honey

Marinate Ahi steaks in the teriyaki sauce for 4 hours.

Remove skins from tomatillos. Place in a food processor with the apple. Chop very fine. Place in a bowl and add remaining ingredients.

Preheat grill or barbecue. Remove fish from marinade. Grill fish until cooked through, about 5 minutes per side (time varies with thickness of fish and type of grill). Serve with relish. If you prefer a spicy relish, add finely diced jalapeños to your taste.

Entrees

PASTA WITH PESTO SAUCE

Serves 4

1½ cups fresh basil
¼ cup pine nuts
¼ cup walnuts
¾ cup grated parmesan cheese
3 cloves garlic
1 cup olive oil
salt and pepper
¾ lb. linguine pasta

Remove stems from basil. Wash and dry basil. Combine basil, nuts, cheese and garlic in a food processor with steel blade. Begin to process and immediately start adding the olive oil, in a slow steady stream, until it has all been added. Scrape down sides, add salt and pepper to taste, and process for about 1 minute more. Set aside.

Cook the pasta al dente. Drain well. Combine the pasta and sauce in a large mixing bowl and toss to coat. Serve immediately.

Coney Glade was named for the many Rock Coneys that live there.

Entrees

PARMESAN CHICKEN

½ cup grated parmesan cheese
½ cup dry bread crumbs
1 teaspoon parsley
1 teaspoon oregano
¼ teaspoon black pepper
¼ teaspoon paprika
4 boneless skinless chicken breasts
3 tablespoons butter or olive oil
1 clove garlic, crushed

Mix cheese, bread crumbs, herbs and spices in a shallow dish. Set aside.

Melt butter. Add garlic and sauté for a few minutes. Dip chicken breasts, one at a time, first in the butter, then in the crumb mixture. Set on a baking pan. Bake at 400 degrees for 15-20 minutes, until cooked through.

Entrees

TOMATO BEEF CHOW MEIN

Serves 4-6

¾ lb. flank steak
2 teaspoons cornstarch
2 teaspoons soy sauce
1 tablespoon sherry
2 tablespoons cornstarch
½ cup catsup
½ cup chicken broth
2 tablespoons oyster sauce
1 tablespoon peanut oil
1 onion, cut into eighths
2 stalks celery, sliced diagonally
1 green pepper, chopped
2 tomatoes, diced
4 cups chow mein noodles

Slice the flank steak thinly across the grain. Mix 2 teaspoons cornstarch, 2 teaspoons soy sauce and 1 tablespoon sherry, and toss with the steak. Set aside to marinate for 30 minutes. Meanwhile whisk together the 2 tablespoons cornstarch, catsup, broth and oyster sauce in a small bowl and set aside.

In a wok or large skillet, heat the peanut oil. Stir-fry the onion, celery and peppers until just tender. Remove from pan. Stir-fry the beef until done medium rare. Add sauce mixture, tomatoes and vegetables. Cook until thick. Serve over chow mein noodles.

Entrees

PORK MEDALLIONS IN MUSTARD SAUCE

Serves 8

2¼ lb. pork tenderloin
½ cup flour
4 tablespoons butter
⅓ cup red wine vinegar
8 crushed peppercorns
2 cups heavy cream
½ cup Dijon mustard
2 tablespoons butter
½ teaspoon salt

Slice tenderloin into thin slices. Dredge in flour. Melt 2 tablespoons butter in large frying pan, and sauté the tenderloin in batches, adding the additional butter as needed. Set pork aside, covered. Add vinegar and peppercorns to pan. Boil until reduced by ⅔. Add cream, and simmer 5 minutes. Remove from heat and add remaining ingredients. Spoon over pork on individual plates.

Entrees

HUMMUS PITAS

Makes 6 sandwiches

Hummus:
1 15 oz. can garbanzo beans
½ cup tahini (sesame paste)
½ cup fresh lemon juice
2 cloves garlic
2-3 tablespoons water
salt and pepper

6 pita breads
1 tomato, diced
1 cup shredded lettuce
½ cup shredded carrots
1 cup alfalfa sprouts

Combine all hummus ingredients in a food processor, except salt and pepper. Blend until smooth. Season to taste with salt and pepper. Spread each pita bread with the hummus. Add tomatoes, lettuce, carrots and sprouts. Fold in half and serve. The hummus mixture can also be used as a dip for crackers.

Sometimes I leave my skis behind and venture for a hike up the frosty mountainside to my destination, Dudley's. The birds singing and the freshly scented pines along the way are most enlivening.

-Gayle Shugars

Entrees

LINGUINE WITH SMOKED CHICKEN AND GREEN CHILE PESTO

Serves 6

¾ cup diced green chiles
1 small chipotle chile
¼ cup grated parmesan cheese
¼ cup pine nuts
¼ cup packed fresh cilantro
1 clove garlic
juice of ½ lime
3 tablespoons olive oil
1 pound linguine
1 cup shredded smoked chicken breast
1 tomato, diced

Make pesto: Place chiles, cheese, nuts, cilantro, garlic and lime juice in food processor. Process 30 seconds. Slowly add the olive oil while the machine is running. Scrape down the sides of the bowl and process 10 seconds more. Set aside.

Bring a large pot of water to a boil. Cook linguine until al dente. Drain. Toss with pesto, chicken and tomatoes and serve immediately.

Entrees

MAHOGANY CHICKEN

Serves 6-8

1½ cups soy sauce
¾ cup sherry
1 cup hoisin sauce
¾ cup plum sauce
12 green onions, chopped
6 cloves garlic, minced
¾ cup cider vinegar
½ cup honey
4 lbs. chicken parts

Combine first 8 ingredients in a large pot and bring to a boil. Add chicken parts. Simmer until chicken is cooked through, about 1 hour. Serve with white rice.

Entrees

BARBECUED PORK SANDWICHES

Makes 6-8 sandwiches.

1 3-lb. boneless pork roast
salt and pepper
Kaiser rolls

Sauce:
½ tablespoon olive oil
1 small onion, diced
2 cloves garlic, chopped
¼ cup Jack Daniels
¼ cup strong coffee
2 cups ketchup
¼ cup molasses
¼ cup brown sugar
¼ cup worcestershire sauce
¼ cup tomato paste
¼ cup water
½ cup apple cider vinegar
1 tablespoon liquid smoke
2 teaspoons chili powder
juice of 1 lime

Sprinkle the pork roast with salt and pepper. Bake at 325 degrees for about two hours, until a meat thermometer registers 160 degrees.

Meanwhile, prepare the sauce: In a medium saucepan, sauté the onion until soft. Add garlic and cook another minute. Add Jack Daniels and cook a few minutes. Add all remaining ingredients and bring to a boil. Pour ½ the sauce into a large baking dish. When the roast is done, let cool slightly, then slice thinly and place the sliced meat in the sauce. Pour remaining sauce over. Cover the pan with foil and return to oven for 1 hour, gently stirring occasionally. Serve on Kaiser rolls, spooning extra sauce over.

Entrees

MEATLOAF

This recipe makes a very dense loaf, so any leftovers will slice beautifully for sandwiches.

Serves 8-10

2½ lbs. ground beef
1 cup bread crumbs
¾ cup grated parmesan cheese
¾ cup milk
1 cup diced onions
2 eggs
1 tablespoon garlic salt
1 tablespoon worcestershire sauce
1 teaspoon each: black pepper, thyme, sage

Preheat oven to 350 degrees. Combine all ingredients in a large mixing bowl and mix thoroughly. Pack into a greased loaf pan and bake for 1 hour and 15 minutes. Remove from pan and let sit 5 minutes before slicing. Serve hot with mashed potatoes and steamed vegetables, or use hot or cold for meatloaf sandwiches.

Sam's Knob was named after local rancher Sam Stapleton, who used to run cattle and sheep on the part of Snowmass Mountain now known as the Knob.

Entrees

SEA BASS WITH LIME-CHIPOTLE SAUCE

This spicy sauce is delicious on any fish, but especially white fish.

Serves 4

½ cup lime juice
3 tablespoons honey
6 cloves garlic
1 chipotle chile in adobo sauce
¼ teaspoon cumin
1 tablespoon tequila
1 teaspoon cornstarch
1 tablespoon cilantro, diced
4 sea bass fillets

Combine first 7 ingredients in a food processor. Process until smooth. Place sauce in a small pan and cook until thickened. Add cilantro.

Preheat broiler. Place fish fillets in a shallow pan. Brush with sauce. Broil about 3-4 minutes. Turn fish over and brush the other side with sauce. Broil 3-4 more minutes, or until done. Garnish fish with slices of lime and fresh cilantro sprigs. Serve additional sauce on the side.

Entrees

GRILLED CHICKEN WITH ORANGE-MUSTARD SAUCE

Serves 4

4 boneless chicken breasts
Marinade:
3 tablespoons orange juice concentrate
2 tablespoons Dijon mustard
2 tablespoons vegetable oil
2 tablespoons honey
2 tablespoons soy sauce
1 clove garlic, crushed

Sauce:
3 tablespoons orange juice concentrate
3 tablespoons apricot jam
2 tablespoons Dijon mustard
2 tablespoons lemon juice

Place the chicken breasts in a shallow dish. Combine the marinade ingredients in a small bowl and pour over the chicken. Cover and refrigerate several hours or overnight.

Meanwhile, combine all sauce ingredients in a small pan and bring to a boil. Keep warm, or reheat when ready to use.

Preheat grill or broiler. Remove chicken breasts from the marinade and grill for about 3 minutes per side. Serve with sauce, and garnish with orange slices.

Entrees

CAJUN CHICKEN SANDWICHES

For a light supper, serve the chicken breast, sliced, on a bed of mixed greens. Sundried tomato vinaigrette would be a good choice of dressing.

Serves 4

2 tablespoons paprika
1 teaspoon salt
1 teaspoon onion powder
1 teaspoon garlic powder
1 teaspoon cayenne pepper
½ teaspoon white pepper
½ teaspoon black pepper
½ teaspoon thyme
½ teaspoon oregano
4 skinless, boneless chicken breasts
4 whole grain hamburger buns
sliced tomatoes
lettuce
mayonnaise

Preheat barbecue grill on medium-high setting. Combine all spices in a shallow pan. Dip each chicken breast in the spice mixture to lightly coat both sides. Grill 3-4 minutes per side, or just until done. Serve on toasted buns with lettuce, tomatoes and mayonnaise.

Entrees

STEW

Serves 8

1½ lbs. stew meat
4 cups water
2 cups potatoes, chopped
1 cup carrots, chopped
1 cup celery, chopped
½ cup onions, chopped
¾ teaspoon each: garlic salt, black pepper, basil, marjoram and thyme
½ cup red wine
1 beef bouillon cube
2 tablespoons tomato paste
2 bay leaves
2 tablespoons cornstarch dissolved in ¼ cup cold water

Brown meat in oil. Add water. Simmer 2 hours. Add potatoes, carrots, celery, and onions, and simmer for 1 more hour. Then add spices, red wine, beef bouillon, tomato paste, bay leaves, and cornstarch/water and cook for 20 minutes, or until tender.

Entrees

SPINACH BURGERS

1 lb. frozen chopped spinach (thawed and drained)
3 egg whites (beat with fork first)
1 cup bread crumbs
⅓ cup romano cheese
⅓ teaspoon cumin
½ teaspoon garlic salt
3 tablespoons diced onions

Preheat oven to 350 degrees. Mix together all ingredients. Form into patties and place on a greased cookie sheet. Bake for 10 minutes. Serve on a bun like a burger. Try it with cheese or salsa on top.

Entrees

TURKEY TARRAGON BURGERS

This recipe can also be used for meatballs or meatloaf; just change the shape.

Serves 6

1 pound ground turkey
½ cup finely diced onion
¼ cup whole wheat bread crumbs
2½ tablespoons chopped parsley
½ teaspoon thyme
¼ teaspoon salt
½ teaspoon pepper
1 egg white
½ tablespoon olive oil
¼ cup flour
2 tablespoons chopped fresh tarragon
½ cup white wine
hamburger buns and garnishes

Combine the first 8 ingredients in a medium bowl and mix thoroughly. Form the meat mixture into 6 patties. Heat the olive oil in a non-stick skillet. Dredge the patties in the flour and place them in the skillet. Cook 5 minutes on each side. Add the tarragon and the wine and continue cooking until the wine is reduced to just a few tablespoons.

Place the patties on toasted buns, spoon the reduced wine over and garnish as desired.

Entrees

ORIENTAL SWORDFISH

Serves 4

⅓ cup olive oil
1 tablespoon sesame oil
juice of 1 lime
1 tablespoon chopped cilantro
4 swordfish steaks

Sauce:
¼ cup sherry vinegar
¼ cup soy sauce
½ teaspoon salt
6 tablespoons sesame oil
6 tablespoons vegetable oil

Combine the first 4 ingredients. Place the swordfish in a shallow dish and pour the marinade over. Cover and refrigerate 2 to 3 hours. To make the sauce, place the first 4 ingredients in a food processor. Turn on the machine and slowly add the oils. Process 10 seconds. Set aside.

Remove the swordfish from the marinade and grill or broil about 3 minutes per side, or until just cooked through. Serve with the sauce poured over the top and garnish with lime slices.

Cookies and Bars

Cookies

CHOCOLATE CHIP OATMEAL COOKIES

Yield: 20 small cookies

¼ pound butter
½ cup brown sugar
¼ cup white sugar
1 teaspoon vanilla
1 egg
1 tablespoon water
1½ cups oatmeal
1¼ cups flour
1 teaspoon cinnamon
¼ teaspoon baking soda
½ teaspoon salt
½ cup chocolate chips
¼ cup raisins

Preheat oven to 350 degrees. Cream butter. Add sugars and beat until light and fluffy. Beat in vanilla, egg, and water. Add remaining ingredients and beat until thoroughly combined.

Drop onto greased cookie sheets by teaspoonfuls. Flatten with wet fingers. Bake for 15 minutes or until very light brown. Remove from pans to cool.

Cookies

HAZELNUT BISCOTTI

Biscotti are hard cookies meant for dipping in coffee. They can be stored in an airtight container for up to a month.

Yield: 4 dozen cookies

2 cups flour
1 cup sugar
1 teaspoon baking powder
3 eggs
2 tablespoons brandy
2 tablespoons Frangellica liqueur
1 teaspoon vanilla
1 cup toasted hazelnuts, coarsely chopped

Preheat oven to 300 degrees. Combine flour, sugar, and baking powder in a bowl or food processor. Whisk together the eggs, brandy, liqueur, and vanilla, and add to the dry mix. Mix well or process about 30 seconds. Mix in the nuts by hand. The mixture will be very sticky.

On a floured surface, form the dough into 2 logs, each about 14 inches long and 1½ inches thick. Place them on a lightly greased cookie sheet and bake for 30 minutes. Remove the logs from the sheets and slice diagonally into ½-inch slices. Stand the cookies upright on the baking sheet and return to the oven for another 30 minutes. Cool before storing.

COCONUT BARS

Yield: 12-24 bars

2 cups flour
1 cup butter
½ cup sugar
2 egg yolks
1 teaspoon vanilla
½ cup apricot jam
¾ cup melted butter
⅓ cup sugar
3 tablespoons water
14 ounces shredded coconut
2 eggs
1 teaspoon vanilla

Preheat oven to 350 degrees. Mix the first 5 ingredients together until the dough sticks together. Press into a greased 9x13 inch pan. Bake for 10 minutes. Spread the apricot jam over the warm base. Set aside.

Mix all remaining ingredients together in a medium bowl. Lightly spread the filling over the jam. Return to the oven for 20 minutes. Cool completely, then cut into the desired size bars.

Cookies

TURTLE BARS

Yield: 12-24 bars

1½ cups flour
1½ cups oatmeal
¾ cup brown sugar
2 teaspoons baking soda
½ teaspoon salt
¾ cup melted butter
½ cup chocolate chips
½ cup pecans
1 cup caramel ice cream topping

Preheat oven to 350 degrees. Combine first 6 ingredients in a food processor until the mixture just begins to clump together. Press ⅔ of the mixture into a greased 9x13 inch pan. Bake for 15 minutes, or until very light brown. Let cool 15 minutes. Sprinkle the base with the chocolate chips and pecans. Drizzle the ice cream topping over that, then crumble the reserved topping over the top. Bake an additional 20 minutes. Let cool before cutting into squares.

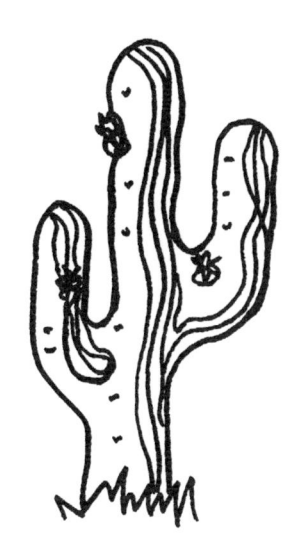

Cookies

FUDGE BROWNIES

Yield: 9 large brownies

½ cup butter
⅓ cup unsweetened cocoa
3 eggs
1 teaspoon vanilla
⅔ cup sugar
⅔ cup brown sugar
¾ cup flour
½ cup chopped walnuts

Preheat the oven to 350 degrees. Grease a 9-inch square pan and set aside. Melt together the butter and cocoa. In a medium bowl, mix the eggs, vanilla, and sugars. Add the butter/cocoa mixture. Stir in the flour and walnuts. Pour the batter into the prepared pan and bake for 20 to 30 minutes, or until a toothpick inserted into the center of the brownies comes out almost dry. Cool before cutting.

Cookies

CHOCOLATE CHIP COOKIES

Yield: 24-30 cookies

1 cup butter
2 ounces vegetable shortening
1 cup brown sugar
¾ cup sugar
2 eggs
1 teaspoon vanilla
¼ teaspoon maple extract
⅛ teaspoon salt
1 teaspoon baking soda
3 cups flour
2 cups chocolate chips

Preheat the oven to 350 degrees. Cream the butter, shortening and sugars together until light. Add eggs and flavorings and mix well. Add all remaining ingredients and mix until well combined. Drop batter by tablespoonfuls onto greased cookie sheets, flattening the cookies slightly with wet fingers. Bake for 10-12 minutes. The centers should be light and puffy. Remove from the oven and cool the cookies on the cookie sheets.

The ski trail named Bonzai Ridge has a beautiful, gnarled, twisted old tree on it, like a giant Bonsai tree.

Cookies

SHORTBREAD COOKIES

Yield: 36 cookies

2 cups flour
½ cup rice flour
1 cup butter
½ cup sugar
¼ teaspoon salt

Preheat the oven to 350 degrees. Place all the ingredients in a mixing bowl and beat until the dough sticks together. Place on a lightly floured surface and roll out to ¼-inch thickness. Cut into bars or any shape desired. Place the cookies on a greased cookie sheet and bake approximately 15 minutes, until nicely browned. Cool before serving.

Cookies

RASPBERRY BARS

Yield: 9 bars

1½ cups flour
10 tablespoons butter
½ cup powdered sugar
¼ teaspoon salt
1 egg
1½ cups fresh or frozen raspberries
½ cup melted butter
1 cup sugar
2 eggs
½ cup toasted hazelnuts, chopped
1 cup shredded coconut

Preheat the oven to 350 degrees. Grease a 9-inch square pan and set aside. Mix the flour, butter, powdered sugar and salt until crumbly. Add the egg and mix until the dough sticks together. Press into the prepared pan. Bake for 15 minutes. Cool slightly.

Sprinkle the raspberries over the crust. Set aside. In a medium bowl, combine all remaining ingredients. Spoon over the raspberries. Bake an additional 30 minutes or until set. Cool before cutting.

Cookies

WHEAT GERM COOKIES

Yield: 20-24 cookies

½ cup butter
½ cup peanut butter
⅓ cup sugar
½ cup brown sugar
1 egg
1 teaspoon baking soda
¼ teaspoon salt
½ cup oatmeal
½ cup wheat germ
⅓ cup coconut
½ cup whole wheat flour
¼ cup raisins

Preheat the oven to 350 degrees. In a mixing bowl, beat together the first 5 ingredients until light. Add the remaining ingredients and mix well. Drop the batter by tablespoonfuls onto greased cookie sheets. Bake for 15 minutes, or until golden brown. Allow the cookies to cool on the sheets.

Cookies

DATE BARS

Yield: 9 bars

2 cups flour
⅔ cup sugar
1 cup butter, softened
3 cups dates
1 cup sugar
1 cup orange juice
4 tablespoons butter
3 eggs

Preheat the oven to 350 degrees. Mix the first 3 ingredients until crumbly. Press ⅔ of this mixture into a greased 9-inch square pan. Bake for 10 minutes. Cool slightly. Set the remaining crumbs aside.

Mix the remaining ingredients in a saucepan and cook over medium heat, stirring often, until the dates have softened, about 10 minutes. Pour the date mixture over the crust. Crumble the remaining crumbs over the top. Return to the oven for 30 minutes. Cool before cutting.

Cookies

OATMEAL COOKIES

Yield: 48 cookies

1 cup butter
1 cup brown sugar
½ cup sugar
1 egg
1 teaspoon vanilla
¾ teaspoon soda
⅛ teaspoon salt
1 teaspoon cinnamon
1½ cups flour
3 cups oatmeal
1½ cups raisins

Preheat the oven to 350 degrees. Cream the butter and sugars until light and fluffy. Add the egg and vanilla and mix well. Add all remaining ingredients and mix thoroughly. Drop the batter by teaspoonfuls onto greased cookie sheets. Flatten cookies with wet fingers. Bake about 12-15 minutes, or until very light brown.

Cookies

PEANUT BUTTER COOKIES

Yield: 30-36 cookies

1 cup butter
1 cup peanut butter
¾ cup brown sugar
¾ cup sugar
2 eggs
1 teaspoon vanilla
¼ teaspoon salt
½ teaspoon baking soda
2¼ cups flour

Preheat the oven to 350 degrees. In a mixing bowl, cream the butter, peanut butter and sugars until light and fluffy. Add the eggs and vanilla and mix well. Add all remaining ingredients and mix thoroughly. Drop batter by tablespoonfuls onto greased cookie sheets. Flatten with wet fingers or with the tines of a fork. Bake for 12-15 minutes, or until golden brown. Cool on the cookie sheets.

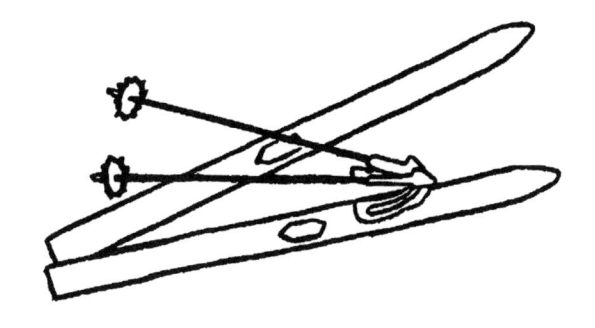

Cookies

TRIPLE CHUNK COOKIES

Yield: 20 cookies

4 ounces semisweet chocolate
4 ounces unsweetened chocolate
½ cup butter
2 eggs
1 cup sugar
1 teaspoon vanilla
¼ teaspoon salt
1 teaspoon baking powder
½ cup flour
⅓ cup chocolate chips
⅓ cup chopped pecans or walnuts
4 ounces white chocolate, chopped

Preheat the oven to 350 degrees. Melt the semisweet and unsweetened chocolates and the butter together in a double boiler or microwave. Cool slightly. In a medium bowl, whisk together the eggs, sugar, and vanilla. Add the chocolate mixture and whisk until combined. Add the remaining ingredients and stir until all of the flour is incorporated. Drop by tablespoonfuls onto greased cookie sheets. Bake for 10 minutes. Remove from the pans to cool.

Desserts

Desserts

BLACKBERRY COBBLER

Serves 9

4 cups blackberries, fresh or frozen
½ cup sugar
2 tablespoons cornstarch
1¾ cups flour
3 tablespoons sugar
1½ teaspoons baking powder
⅛ teaspoon salt
3 tablespoons butter
1 egg
⅔ cup milk

Preheat oven to 350 degrees. Grease a 9-inch square baking pan. In a medium bowl, toss the berries with the ½ cup sugar and cornstarch. Place mixture in the prepared pan and set aside.

Combine the flour, sugar, baking powder, and salt in a medium bowl. Cut in the butter until crumbly. Mix the egg and the milk together in a separate bowl, then stir into the dry mixture until just moistened. Drop the batter by large spoonfuls to form 9 equal mounds on top of the fruit. Bake the cobbler until the fruit bubbles and the biscuits are done, about 45 minutes. Serve warm, with whipped cream or vanilla ice cream.

Desserts

PEACH-BLUEBERRY CRISP

Serves 12

10 cups sliced peaches, fresh or frozen
2 cups blueberries, fresh or frozen
1 cup sugar
4 tablespoons cornstarch
1 cup brown sugar
1 cup butter, melted
1½ cups flour
½ cup oatmeal
1 teaspoon cinnamon

Preheat oven to 350 degrees. Grease a 9x13 inch baking pan. In a large bowl, toss together the fruit, sugar, and cornstarch. Arrange the fruit mixture in the prepared pan.

In a medium bowl, combine the remaining ingredients and stir with a wooden spoon until the mixture is crumbly. Distribute the topping evenly over the fruit. Bake for 1 hour, or until the fruit begins to bubble around the edges. Cool partially before serving. Top with whipped cream or vanilla ice cream.

> *Living and working up at Dudley's on Sam's Knob will always bring back good memories for me. Nothing can compare to the view I had while tending bar. I also loved the afternoon walks around the Knob once the skiers were off the mountain. This is a special place.*
>
> *-Lea Mowan*

Desserts

PIE CRUST

Yield: one double crust or 2 single crusts

3 cups flour
½ teaspoon salt
12 tablespoons cold butter
12 tablespoons shortening
1 teaspoon vinegar
1 egg
5 to 6 tablespoons cold water

Process the flour and salt in a food processor for 20 seconds. Cut the butter into small pieces and distribute them over the flour. Add the shortening and process the mixture until it resembles coarse meal, about 20 seconds. In a small bowl, whisk together the vinegar, egg, and 5 tablespoons of water. With the food processor running, pour the mixture through the feed tube and process until the dough sticks together. Add the additional tablespoon of water if needed. Turn out the dough onto a lightly floured surface and knead a few times. Divide into 2 pieces and roll out. Chill before filling or baking.

Fast Draw got its name because it is a fast, narrow, direct route off the Knob.

Desserts

PEANUT BUTTER PIE

Serves 8-10

Crust:
⅓ cup butter
6 ounces semisweet chocolate
1½ cups Rice Krispies

Filling:
8 ounces cream cheese, softened
¾ cup peanut butter
14-ounce can sweetened condensed milk
1 teaspoon vanilla
¾ cup heavy cream
½ cup fudge ice cream topping

For the crust, melt the butter and chocolate together in a double boiler or microwave. Stir in the Rice Krispies until coated. Press into a greased 9-inch pie pan. Set aside.

In a medium bowl, beat the cream cheese and the peanut butter together until fluffy. Add the condensed milk and the vanilla and mix well. In a separate bowl, whip the heavy cream until stiff. Fold into the peanut butter mixture. Pour into the crust. Drizzle the fudge sauce over the top, and with a knife, swirl it through the pie. Cover and chill overnight. Garnish with whipped cream, nuts, and chocolate sauce, if desired.

Desserts

LOWFAT LEMON CHEESE PIE

Serves 8

Crust:
1½ cups graham cracker crumbs
2 tablespoons sugar
4 tablespoons melted butter

Filling:
1 envelope unflavored gelatin
⅓ cup orange juice
2 cups lowfat cottage cheese
¼ cup apple juice concentrate
2 tablespoons honey
3 egg whites
1 teaspoon vanilla
2 tablespoons lemon juice
grated rind of ½ lemon
sliced fruit for garnish

Preheat the oven to 350 degrees. Mix all the crust ingredients together in a small bowl. Press into a 9-inch tart pan. Bake for 10 minutes. Set aside.

For the filling, sprinkle the gelatin over the orange juice in a small saucepan. Let soften for 1 minute, then heat until the gelatin dissolves. Set aside. Place the cottage cheese in a food processor and process until it is very smooth. Add the gelatin and the remaining filling ingredients and process briefly. Pour filling into the crust and chill several hours or overnight. Garnish with fresh fruit before serving.

Desserts

WHITE CHOCOLATE TART

Serves 8-10

Crust:
¾ cup ground toasted almonds
¾ cup graham cracker crumbs
3 tablespoons sugar
4 tablespoons melted butter

Filling:
10 ounces white chocolate
8 tablespoons butter
1½ cups heavy cream
2 tablespoons Grand Marnier liqueur
1 teaspoon vanilla
1 egg white
fresh fruit for garnish

Preheat oven to 350 degrees. Combine the crust ingredients in a small bowl and mix until combined. Press into a 9-inch pie pan. Bake for 10 minutes, then set aside to cool while you make the filling.

Chop the white chocolate into small pieces. Melt the chocolate and the butter in the top of a double boiler. Remove from the heat. Stir in ½ cup of the heavy cream, the liqueur, and the vanilla. Whip the remaining cream until stiff, and fold into the filling. Whip the egg white until stiff and fold in. Pour the filling into the shell and chill for several hours or overnight. Garnish with fresh fruit.

Desserts

CHOCOLATE BANANA SPLIT PIE

Serves 8

one 9-inch pie shell, baked

Chocolate layer:
5 tablespoons butter
3 ounces semisweet chocolate
⅓ cup sugar
1 egg
1 teaspoon vanilla
4 tablespoons flour

Custard:
1¼ cups milk
1 teaspoon gelatin
¼ cup sugar
3 egg yolks
1 tablespoon cornstarch
1 teaspoon vanilla
2 tablespoons butter

2 bananas
8 to 10 strawberries
1 cup sweetened whipped cream

Preheat oven to 350 degrees. To make the chocolate layer, melt the chocolate and butter together in a double boiler or microwave. Set aside. In a medium bowl, beat together the remaining ingredients, then add the chocolate and mix until smooth. Pour into the crust and bake for 10 minutes. Chill completely.

Desserts

To make the custard, place the milk, gelatin, and sugar in a saucepan, and let sit for 5 minutes. Meanwhile, whisk together the egg yolks and cornstarch. Cook the milk mixture until it comes to a boil. Pour a small amount of the hot mixture into the egg mixture, then return that to the saucepan. Cook, stirring constantly, until the mixture boils and thickens. Remove from the heat. Whisk in the vanilla and butter. Cool slightly.

To assemble, slice the bananas over the chocolate layer, then spoon the custard over. Chill several hours. Top with sliced strawberries and whipped cream. This is a very impressive dessert!

Desserts

CHOCOLATE BOURBON PECAN PIE

Serves 8-10

one 9-inch pie shell, unbaked
1½ cups pecan halves
4 ounces unsweetened chocolate
6 tablespoons butter
5 eggs
1 cup sugar
¾ cup dark corn syrup
¼ cup bourbon
1 teaspoon vanilla

Preheat the oven to 350 degrees. Place the pecan halves in the pie crust and set aside.

Melt the chocolate and the butter in a double boiler or microwave. Set aside. In a medium bowl, whisk the eggs. Add the remaining ingredients and the chocolate mixture and stir until smooth. Pour the filling over the pecans. Carefully place the pie in the preheated oven and bake until puffed up and set, about one hour. Cool completely. Serve with sweetened whipped cream with a splash of bourbon added.

Desserts

KEY LIME PIE

Serves 8

Crust:
1 cup graham cracker crumbs
½ cup shredded coconut
¼ cup sugar
4 tablespoons butter, melted

Filling:
5 large egg yolks
14-ounce can sweetened condensed milk
¾ cup plain yogurt
½ cup key lime juice

Garnish:
1 cup heavy cream
¼ cup sugar
lime slices
toasted coconut

Preheat the oven to 350 degrees. Mix all crust ingredients in a small bowl, then press into a 9-inch pie pan. Bake 10 minutes. Set aside.

In a medium bowl, whisk the egg yolks. Add the sweetened condensed milk and the yogurt and whisk until thoroughly combined. Whisk in the lime juice. Pour into the crust and bake for 15 minutes. Chill several hours or overnight.

Just before serving, whip the cream and the sugar until stiff. Pipe or spread on the pie, and garnish with lime slices and toasted coconut.

Desserts

PUMPKIN PIE

Serves 8

one 9-inch pie shell, unbaked
1½ cups pumpkin
¾ cup brown sugar
4 eggs
½ teaspoon salt
1 teaspoon cinnamon
1 teaspoon ginger
¼ teaspoon nutmeg
1½ cups evaporated milk
¼ cup Kahlua

Preheat the oven to 400 degrees. In a medium bowl, whisk the pumpkin, brown sugar, and eggs until smooth. Add remaining ingredients and whisk until thoroughly combined. Carefully pour the mixture into the pie crust and place in the preheated oven. Bake at 400 degrees for 15 minutes, then reduce the heat to 350 degrees and bake until set in the center, about 30 or 40 minutes longer. Cool before serving, and garnish with sweetened whipped cream.

Lunchline got its name because it takes people into Lift #3 and back up to the Sam's Knob Restaurant.

Desserts

OATMEAL FUDGE CAKE

Serves 12

Cake:
6 ounces semisweet chocolate
6 ounces butter
1½ cups oatmeal
1¾ cups boiling water
4 eggs
1¾ cups sugar
1 teaspoon baking soda
½ teaspoon baking powder
½ teaspoon salt
2¼ cups flour

Topping:
12 tablespoons soft butter
¾ cup heavy cream
1½ cups brown sugar
1½ cups chopped pecans
2 cups shredded coconut

Preheat the oven to 350 degrees. Chop the chocolate and the butter into 1-inch pieces and place in a medium bowl with the oatmeal and the boiling water. Let sit for 10 minutes, or until the chocolate has melted. Add the remaining cake ingredients and mix well. Pour batter into a greased 9x13-inch cake pan. Bake for 30 minutes, or until the cake tests done. Cool for 15 minutes.

Place all topping ingredients in a bowl and mix well. Spread over the cake and place under the broiler until nicely browned.

Desserts

CHOCOLATE CHUNK BAILEY'S CHEESECAKE

Serves 12-16

Crust:
1¼ cups vanilla wafer crumbs
5 tablespoons melted butter
1 tablespoon sugar

Filling:
2 pounds cream cheese, softened
1 cup sugar
4 large eggs
2 egg yolks
½ cup Bailey's Irish Cream liqueur
½ cup sour cream
6 ounces semisweet chocolate

Topping:
1 cup sour cream
2 tablespoons sugar
1 teaspoon vanilla

Preheat the oven to 350 degrees. Mix all the crust ingredients and press into the bottom of a 9-inch springform pan. Set aside. In a medium bowl, beat the cream cheese and the sugar until fluffy, scraping down the sides of the bowl several times. Add the eggs and beat 30 seconds. Stir in the liqueur and the sour cream. Chop the chocolate into 1/2-inch chunks and stir into the batter. Pour the batter into the crust and bake until set, about 1 hour.

Mix the topping ingredients in a small bowl. Gently spread the topping over the warm cake, then return it to the oven for 5 minutes. Cool completely, then refrigerate overnight before serving.

Desserts

PEGGY'S NEW YORK STYLE CHEESECAKE

Serves 12-16

2 pounds cream cheese
1½ cups sugar
½ cup cornstarch
8 ounces of butter, melted
2 cups heavy cream
6 eggs

Have all ingredients at room temperature before starting. Preheat oven to 350 degrees. Butter a 10-inch springform pan. Set aside. In a medium bowl, beat the cream cheese and the sugar until light and fluffy, scraping the sides of the bowl often. Add the remaining ingredients one at a time, beating until smooth. Pour into the prepared pan. Place the pan in a shallow baking pan with 1 inch of water in it. Place in the oven and bake for one hour, until set. Cool at room temperature for 3 hours, then refrigerate overnight before serving.

Desserts

CHOCOLATE TRUFFLE CAKE

Serves 12-16

1 pound bittersweet or semisweet chocolate
1 pound butter
6 eggs

Preheat the oven to 400 degrees. Chop the chocolate into small chunks. Place the chocolate and the butter in the top of a double boiler and melt over low heat. Set aside.

Place the eggs in a stainless steel bowl that fits over the bottom of the double boiler. Increase the heat to medium, and cook for 10 minutes, while beating the eggs with an electric mixer. The eggs will be thick and light colored. Remove the bowl from the heat. Stir in the melted chocolate mixture. Pour the batter into a greased 9-inch springform pan. Bake for 15 minutes. Let cool, then refrigerate overnight.

Garnish with sweetened whipped cream and strawberries.

Desserts

TROPICAL BANANA CAKE

Serves 12-14

¾ cup butter
1¼ cups sugar
2 eggs
2¼ cups flour
1 teaspoon baking powder
½ teaspoon baking soda
¼ teaspoon salt
⅔ cup buttermilk
1 cup mashed bananas
1 teaspoon vanilla
½ cup chopped pecans
1½ cups shredded coconut
one recipe cream cheese icing (see index)

Preheat oven to 350 degrees. Grease 2 9-inch layer cake pans. Cream the butter and sugar until fluffy. Add the eggs and beat for one minute, scraping the sides of the bowl. Combine the flour, baking powder, soda, and salt in a separate bowl. Add ½ of this dry mixture to the batter and mix on low speed. Add the bananas, buttermilk, and the vanilla. Add the remaining dry mixture and mix for 30 seconds. Fold in the pecans and 1 cup of the coconut. Pour into the prepared pans and bake until the cakes test done, about 20 minutes. Remove the layers from the pans to cool.

Toast the remaining ½ cup coconut in the oven until golden brown. When the cakes are cool, frost with cream cheese icing and sprinkle with the toasted coconut.

Desserts

CITRUS TART

Serves 8-10

Crust:
1 ¼ cups flour
2 tablespoons sugar
¼ teaspoon salt
½ cup butter
1 egg yolk
1 tablespoon cold water

Filling:
½ cup heavy cream
2 tablespoons cornstarch
2 eggs
6 egg yolks
¾ cup sugar
¾ cup fresh lemon juice
½ cup orange juice
¼ cup butter

To make the crust, combine the first 3 ingredients in a food processor. Cut in the butter until crumbly. Add the egg yolk and water and process until the dough begins to stick together. Wrap the dough in plastic and refrigerate 20 minutes. Roll dough out onto a lightly floured surface to a 13-inch round. Press into a greased 9-inch tart pan and trim the edges. Freeze for one hour. Preheat the oven to 400 degrees. Line the tart shell with foil and weights and bake for 15 minutes. Remove the weights and bake for another 10 minutes, or until golden brown. Set aside.

To make the filling, whisk the cornstarch and the heavy cream in a small bowl. Add the eggs and egg yolks and set aside. Place all remaining ingredients in a heavy saucepan and bring to a boil. When the butter has melted, remove from the heat. Whisk a small amount of the hot mixture into the egg mixture, then add the egg mixture to the saucepan. Bring to a boil again, then remove from the heat. Cool slightly, then pour the filling into the crust and chill overnight. Serve garnished with fresh berries.

Desserts

FRENCH SILK PIE

Serves 8

one 8-inch chocolate crumb pie crust
¾ cup butter
1 cup sugar
6 tablespoons unsweetened cocoa
5 eggs

Have the butter and eggs at room temperature before starting. In a medium bowl, cream the butter and sugar together until light and fluffy. Beat in the cocoa. Add the eggs, one at a time, beating a full 5 minutes after each. A tabletop mixer makes this much easier. Spoon the filling into the pie crust and chill overnight. Garnish with sweetened whipped cream and chocolate shavings.

Desserts

CHOCOLATE DREAM PIE

Serves 8

one 8-inch chocolate crumb crust
4½ ounces unsweetened chocolate
5 tablespoons butter
3 eggs, separated
¾ cup sugar
2 tablespoons brewed espresso
2 tablespoons brandy
½ cup heavy cream

Chop the chocolate into small pieces and place in the top of a double boiler with the butter. Melt over medium heat. Remove from the heat and set aside. In a stainless steel bowl, place the egg yolks, sugar, espresso and brandy. Set over the double boiler and beat for 10 minutes over medium-high heat. Remove the bowl from the double boiler. Add the melted chocolate and stir until smooth. In a separate bowl, whip the egg whites until stiff and fold into the chocolate mixture. Whip the heavy cream until stiff and fold that in also. Spoon the filling into the crust and chill overnight. Let sit at room temperature for 30 minutes before serving for the best flavor. Garnish with sweetened whipped cream and a few sliced strawberries.

Desserts

CHOCOLATE CHIP PIE

Serves 8

one 9-inch unbaked pie crust
1 cup butter, melted
6 eggs
½ cup sugar
1 teaspoon vanilla
1¼ cups flour
2 cups walnuts
2 cups chocolate chips

Preheat the oven to 350 degrees. Place the butter, eggs, sugar and vanilla in a medium bowl and mix well. Add the remaining ingredients and stir until thoroughly combined. Pour the filling into the unbaked pie shell. Bake for 45 minutes, or until set. Let cool at room temperature for several hours before serving.

Desserts

PECAN PIE

Serves 8

one 9-inch unbaked pie crust
1 cup pecan halves
6 eggs
3 ounces butter, melted
½ cup brown sugar
1 cup dark corn syrup
1 teaspoon vanilla

Preheat the oven to 350 degrees. Arrange the pecan halves in the bottom of the pie crust. Combine all remaining ingredients in a mixing bowl and whisk until combined. Carefully pour the filling over the pecans. Place the pie in the preheated oven and bake for one hour, or until set. Cool before serving.

Desserts

HOT FUDGE SUNDAES

Serves 4-6

¼ cup butter
¾ cup heavy cream
½ cup sugar
½ cup brown sugar
¾ cup unsweetened cocoa
2 tablespoons Kahlua liqueur
1 quart vanilla or coffee ice cream
whipped cream and nuts for garnish

In a heavy saucepan, melt the butter. Add the heavy cream, sugars and cocoa and whisk over medium heat until the mixture boils. Remove from the heat and stir in the liqueur. At this point, you can make the sundaes or you can place the hot fudge sauce in a jar and store it in the refrigerator until needed, up to a month. Gently reheat the sauce before using. Garnish your sundaes with sweetened whipped cream and nuts.

Desserts

CARROT CAKE

Serves 12

3 eggs
¾ cup vegetable oil
½ cup sugar
¼ cup brown sugar
¾ cup pineapple juice
2½ cups flour
2 teaspoons baking soda
½ teaspoon salt
2 teaspoons cinnamon
1 cup shredded coconut
1 cup chopped walnuts
2 cups grated carrots

Icing:
½ pound cream cheese, softened
¼ pound butter, softened
3 cups powdered sugar
1 teaspoon vanilla
1 to 2 tablespoons milk

Preheat oven to 350 degrees. In a large mixing bowl, combine all cake ingredients and mix well. Pour batter into a greased 9x13-inch cake pan. Bake about 45 minutes, or until the cake tests done. Cool.

For the icing, beat the cream cheese and butter together until fluffy. Add the powdered sugar and vanilla and continue beating. Add milk until the desired consistency is reached. Frost the cooled cake and serve.

Desserts

PECAN-CHOCOLATE TART

Serves 6-8

2 cups ground pecans
¼ cup brown sugar
¼ teaspoon cinnamon
2 tablespoons melted butter
12 ounces semisweet chocolate
1 cup heavy cream
2 tablespoons sugar

Preheat oven to 350 degrees. Lightly grease a 9-inch tart pan with a removable bottom. In a small bowl, mix the first 4 ingredients until combined. Press into the bottom and up the sides of the tart pan. Bake for 10 minutes. Set aside.

To make the filling, chop the chocolate into small pieces. Melt the chocolate and ½ cup of the cream together in a double boiler or microwave. Stir until smooth, then spread the chocolate mixture into the crust. Cool.

If you're not serving the tart the same day, refrigerate until about an hour before serving. Then before serving, whip the remaining ½ cup cream with the sugar until fairly stiff. Spread or pipe the cream over the tart. Sprinkle with chocolate shavings if desired.

Desserts

YAM-PECAN PIE

Serves 8

1 cup cooked, mashed yams
¼ cup brown sugar
1 egg
1 tablespoon heavy cream
1 tablespoon melted butter
1 teaspoon vanilla
¼ teaspoon salt
½ teaspoon cinnamon
⅛ teaspoon allspice
⅛ teaspoon nutmeg
½ cup sugar
¾ cup corn syrup
3 eggs
1 tablespoon melted butter
¾ cup pecan halves
one 9-inch unbaked pie shell

Preheat the oven to 375 degrees. In a medium bowl, mix the first 10 ingredients. Spoon into the pie shell. Set aside. Mix the sugar, corn syrup, eggs, and melted butter. Stir in the pecans. Pour over the bottom layer in the pie shell. Place in the oven and bake until set, about 1 hour. Cool before serving.

Desserts

APPLE CARAMEL PIE

Serves 10-12

1½ cups flour
⅓ cup sugar
¼ teaspoon salt
½ cup butter
4 ounces cream cheese
3 egg yolks
4 cups apples, peeled and sliced
2 cups heavy cream
5 eggs
1 cup brown sugar
½ teaspoon cinnamon
½ cup sugar
1 cup flour
½ cup butter

Preheat oven to 350 degrees. Place the first 6 ingredients in a food processor and process until it forms a dough. Knead lightly, then roll out to a 14-inch circle. Place the dough in a greased 9-inch springform pan, bringing the dough up the sides as far as possible. Arrange the apples in the crust.

Mix the cream, eggs, brown sugar and cinnamon until blended. Pour over the apples. Crimp the edges of the dough. Place the pie on a cookie sheet to catch any spills, and bake for 45 minutes. Meanwhile, mix the remaining ingredients until crumbly. Crumble this mixture over the pie and return to the oven for 45 more minutes. Cool for several hours, then refrigerate overnight. Drizzle with caramel ice cream topping before serving.

Desserts

CHOCOLATE MOUSSE

Serves 6

2 cups chocolate chips
1 teaspoon vanilla
1½ cups heavy cream
4 eggs

Place the chocolate chips and vanilla in a food processor. Bring the heavy cream to a boil. With the processor running, pour the hot cream over the chocolate chips. Process until the chips are melted. Separate the eggs. Add the yolks to the processor and process for 10 seconds. Whip the egg whites until stiff. Place the chocolate mixture in a mixing bowl and fold in the egg whites. Spoon into serving dishes or wine glasses and chill well before serving.

Desserts

TRIPLE LAYER FUDGE CAKE

Serves 12

Cake:
1 cup butter
2½ cups water
½ cup unsweetened cocoa
2 eggs
1½ cups sugar
1 teaspoon vanilla
1 cup buttermilk
1½ teaspoons baking soda
2⅓ cups flour

Frosting:
1 cup butter, softened
⅓ cup unsweetened cocoa
4 cups powdered sugar
2-3 tablespoons brewed espresso

Preheat the oven to 350 degrees. Grease three 9-inch round cake pans and line with parchment or waxed paper. Melt the butter in a saucepan. Add the water and cocoa and bring to a boil. In a large bowl, whisk the eggs, sugar, vanilla, buttermilk and baking soda. Alternately add the chocolate mixture and the flour, beating until smooth after each addition. Pour the batter into the prepared pans and bake for about 20 minutes, or until the cakes test done. Remove the cakes from the pans, peel off the paper, and cool.

For the frosting, beat all ingredients together until smooth, adding the espresso as needed. Frost the cooled cake and serve.

Desserts

FLAN

Serves 8

6 tablespoons sugar
5 eggs
1 cup heavy cream
1 cup half & half
½ cup powdered sugar
¼ cup brown sugar
1 teaspoon vanilla

Preheat the oven to 350 degrees. In a small heavy saucepan, cook the 6 tablespoons of sugar until it turns caramel colored. Pour into a greased 9-inch pie plate. Tilt the pie plate to cover the bottom with the sugar. Set aside.

Whisk the eggs in a medium bowl. Add all remaining ingredients and whisk until smooth. Place the pie pan into a larger pan with ½ inch of water in it. Pour the custard through a strainer into the pie plate. Carefully place in the oven, and bake for 1 hour, or until a knife inserted into the center of the custard comes out clean. Cool. Just before serving, place a serving plate upside down over the flan and flip them both over to unmold the flan onto the plate. Cut into 8 wedges.

Desserts

RASPBERRY CREAM PIE

Serves 8

one 9-inch unbaked pie crust

4 cups raspberries, fresh or frozen
1 cup sugar
6 tablespoons flour
1½ cups heavy cream
1 egg
½ teaspoon cinnamon
¼ teaspoon salt

Preheat the oven to 375 degrees. Place the berries in the pie crust and set aside. Combine the remaining ingredients in a bowl and whisk thoroughly. Pour over the berries. Place the pie in the oven and bake for 45 minutes to an hour, or until filling is set. Cool before serving.

Desserts

PINEAPPLE CHEESECAKE

Serves 8

one 9-inch graham cracker pie crust
9-ounce can crushed pineapple
3-ounce package lemon jello
1¼ cups boiling water
3 ounces cream cheese
3 tablespoons sugar
½ teaspoon vanilla
1 cup sour cream

Drain the pineapple, reserving the juice. Dissolve the jello in the boiling water. Add the juice from the canned pineapple. Set aside to cool. Cream the cream cheese, sugar and vanilla. Add ¾ cup of the cooled jello mixture, then stir in the sour cream. Pour into the graham cracker crust. Chill while you prepare the topping.

In a small bowl, mix the pineapple with the remaining jello mixture. When it starts to thicken, spoon over the cheesecake. Chill overnight before serving.

Most people see only one facet of Snowmass - the ski area. Working at Dudley's, I was able to see it before and after the lifts operated. Before the lifts opened for the season, we would ride to work on snowmobiles to prepare for opening day, and ski down in untracked powder. Shadow was always outside to greet the first workers to show up.

-Tina Takacs

Desserts

CREAMY CHEESECAKE

Top this wonderful cheesecake with fresh fruit or a fruit sauce.

Serves 12

2 tablespoons butter, melted
2 tablespoons sugar
1¼ cups graham cracker crumbs
1½ pounds cream cheese, softened
¾ cup sugar
2 eggs
1 cup sour cream
1 teaspoon vanilla
1 cup sour cream
2 tablespoons sugar

Preheat the oven to 350 degrees. Combine the first 3 ingredients and press into the bottom of a 9-inch springform pan. Set aside. In a mixing bowl, beat the cream cheese and the sugar together until very light and fluffy, scraping down the sides of the bowl often. Add the eggs and beat just until combined. Lightly mix in the sour cream and the vanilla. Pour the filling into the crust and bake for 1 hour. Meanwhile, mix the 1 cup sour cream with the 2 tablespoons of sugar. When the cheesecake has baked for one hour, gently spread the sour cream mixture over the top. Return the cake to the oven for 5 minutes. Let cool at room temperature for an hour, then refrigerate overnight.

Desserts

CHOCOLATE HAZELNUT TORTE

Serves 12

5 ounces semisweet chocolate
¼ cup water
1 teaspoon instant coffee
⅔ cup butter, softened
1¼ cups sugar
5 eggs, separated
2 cups toasted hazelnuts, ground

Glaze:
2 ounces semisweet chocolate
¼ cup heavy cream
1 tablespoon butter

Preheat the oven to 350 degrees. Lightly grease a 9-inch springform pan. Chop the chocolate and place in a double boiler with the water and instant coffee. Cook until melted. Set aside. Cream the butter and sugar together until light and fluffy. Add the egg yolks and mix well. Mix in the chocolate and the hazelnuts. In another bowl, with clean beaters, whip the egg whites until stiff. Fold the egg whites into the batter. Pour into the prepared pan and bake 1 hour, or until a toothpick inserted into the center of the cake comes out just slightly wet. Cool thoroughly.

Remove the sides of the springform pan. To make the glaze, microwave all the ingredients together until the chocolate is melted. Stir until smooth. Spoon over the cake, letting the glaze run down the sides. Chill until the glaze is set. Bring to room temperature before serving.

Desserts

THREE-LAYER CHEESECAKE

Serves 12

Layer #1:
½ cup butter
¾ cup sugar
2 eggs
1 tablespoon milk
1 teaspoon vanilla
1 cup flour
½ teaspoon salt
½ teaspoon baking powder

Layer #2:
1 pound cream cheese
1⅓ cups sugar
1 cup sour cream
4 eggs

Layer #3:
2 cups sour cream
4 tablespoons sugar
1 teaspoon vanilla

Preheat oven to 350 degrees. Lightly grease a 9x13-inch cake pan. For the bottom layer, cream the butter and sugar. Add eggs, milk, and vanilla and mix well. Add remaining ingredients and mix. Spread into the bottom of the pan. Set aside.

For layer #2, whip the cream cheese with the sugar until light and fluffy. Add sour cream and eggs and mix lightly. Pour over the bottom layer. Bake 1 hour and 15 minutes. Remove from the oven. Mix the ingredients for layer #3, and gently spread over the warm cake. Return to the oven for 5 minutes. Chill the cake overnight. Serve as is, or with berries on top.

Desserts

APPLE-PECAN PUDDING CAKE

Serves 6-8

1 cup flour
⅔ cup sugar
1½ teaspoons baking powder
⅛ teaspoon salt
½ teaspoon cinnamon
½ cup milk
2½ cups chopped peeled apples
½ cup chopped pecans
¼ cup butter
¾ cup brown sugar
¾ cup boiling water

Preheat the oven to 375 degrees. Lightly grease a 9-inch round cake pan or a 1-quart casserole dish. Place the first 6 ingredients in a bowl and mix until smooth. Stir in the apples and pecans. Spoon into the prepared pan and set aside. Combine the remaining ingredients and stir until the butter is melted. Pour over the batter in the pan. Bake the pudding cake for 35 to 45 minutes, or until set. While still warm, spoon into bowls and top with vanilla ice cream, if desired.

Index

A
Ahi, Grilled with Tomatillo-Apple Relish, 114
Altitude adjustments, 11
Appetizers
   Bruschetta, 26
   Carnival Chicken, 30
   Chile Con Queso, 27
   Crab Toasts, 25
   Guacamole, 24
   Nachos with Black Beans, 28
   Spicy Shrimp with Peanut Sauce, 29
Apple
   Pecan Pudding Cake, 180
   Caramel Apple Pie, 171
   Tomatillo-Apple Relish, 114
Avocado Relish, 68

B
Baguettes, 55
Banana
   Cake, Tropical, 161
   Split Pie, Chocolate, 152
   Walnut Muffins, 51
Barbecue Pork Sandwiches, 122
Bars
   Brownies, 136
   Coconut, 134
   Date, 141
   Raspberry, 139
   Turtle, 135
Bean Salad, Mixed, 78
Beef
   Chili, 45
   Meatloaf, 123
   Stew, 127
   Chowmein, 117
Biscotti, Hazelnut, 133
Bisque, Seafood, 43
Biscuits, Sourdough, 50
Black Beans, Nachos with, 28
Blackberry Cobbler, 146
Blueberry
   Muffins, 60
   -Peach Crisp, 147
Boules, 55
Bran Muffins, 61
Breads
   Baguettes, 55
   Boules, 55
   Braided Egg, 59
   Cinnamon Rolls, 56
   Flour Tortillas, 58
   French, 55
   Fruit, Nut & Vegetable, 66
   Herb Rolls, 48
   Mexican Cornbread, 52
   Potato Caraway, 65
   Zucchini, Fruit & Nut, 66
Breakfast (see pages 16-22)
Brownies, 136
Bruschetta, 26
Burgers
   Spinach, 128
   Turkey Tarragon, 129
Buttermilk Pancakes, 20

C
Caesar Salad, 80
Cajun Chicken Sandwiches, 126
Cakes
   Apple Pecan Pudding Cake, 180
   Carrot, 168
   Chocolate Hazelnut, 178
   Chocolate Truffle, 160
   Fudge, Triple Layer, 173
   Oatmeal Fudge, 157
   Tropical Banana, 161
Carnival Chicken, 30
Carrot
   and Potatoes in Cream, 84
   Cake, 168
   -Sesame Dressing, 75
Cheese
   Enchiladas, 94
   Soup, Potato and, 39
Cheesecakes
   Creamy, 177
   Chocolate Chunk Bailey's, 158
   Lowfat Lemon, 150
   New York Style, 159
   Pineapple, 176
   Three Layer, 179
Chicken
   and Green Chile Soup, 41
   Carnival Chicken, 30
   Chilequiles, 99
   Dijon Soup, 42
   Enchiladas, 94
   Kiev, Southwestern, 105
   Mahogany, 121
   Parmesan, 116
   Pot Pie, 100
   Quesadillas, 97
   Sesame, 113
   Smoked, with Linguine, 120
   Tamale Pie, 95

Index

Tortellini Soup, 40
Tortilla Soup, 34
   with Orange Mustard Sauce, 125
Chile(s)
   Con Queso, 27
   Pesto, Linguine with Smoked Chicken, 120
   Verde, 35
Chilequiles, 99
Chili
   Sam's Knob (Beef), 45
   Vegetarian, 44
Chocolate
   Banana Split Pie, 152
   Bourbon Pecan Pie, 154
   Chip Cookies, 137
   Chip-Oatmeal Cookies, 132
   Chip Pie, 165
   Chunk Bailey's Cheesecake, 158
   Dream Pie, 164
   French Silk Pie, 163
   Hazelnut Torte, 178
   Hot Fudge Sauce, 167
   Icing, 173
   Layer Cake, Fudge, 173
   Mousse, 172
   Oatmeal Fudge Cake, 157
   Pecan Tart, 169
   Tart, White, 151
   Triple Chunk Cookies, 144
   Truffle Cake, 160
Chowmein, Tomato Beef, 117
Chutney Vinaigrette, 76
Cinnamon Rolls, 56
Citrus Tart, 162
Cobbler, Blackberry, 146
Coconut Bars, 134
Coffee Cake, Sour Cream, 64
Cole Slaw, Lowfat, 79
Cookies
   Chocolate Chip, 137
   Chocolate Chip-Oatmeal, 132
   Hazelnut Biscotti, 133
   Oatmeal, 142
   Peanut Butter, 143
   Shortbread, 138
   Triple Chunk, 144
   Wheat Germ, 140
Corn Chowder, 46
Cornbread, Mexican, 52
Corn Cheese Scones, 53
Crab Toasts, 25
Cream of (see soups)

Cream Cheese Icing, 168
Crisp, Peach-Blueberry, 147
Crust, Pie, 148

D

Date Bars, 141
Desserts
   Apple Caramel Pie, 171
   Apple Pecan Pudding Cake, 180
   Blackberry Cobbler, 146
   Carrot Cake, 168
   Chocolate Banana Split Pie, 152
   Chocolate Bourbon Pecan Pie, 154
   Chocolate Chunk Bailey's Cheesecake, 158
   Chocolate Chip Pie, 165
   Chocolate Dream Pie, 164
   Chocolate Hazelnut Torte, 178
   Chocolate Mousse, 172
   Chocolate Truffle Cake, 160
   Citrus Tart, 162
   Creamy Cheesecake, 177
   Flan, 174
   French Silk Pie, 163
   Hot Fudge Sundaes, 167
   Key Lime Pie, 155
   Lowfat Lemon Cheese Pie, 150
   Oatmeal Fudge Cake, 157
   Peach-Blueberry Crisp, 147
   Peanut Butter Pie, 149
   Pecan Chocolate Tart, 169
   Pecan Pie, 166
   Peggy's New York Cheesecake, 159
   Pie Crust, 148
   Pineapple Cheesecake, 176
   Pumpkin Pie, 156
   Raspberry Cream Pie, 175
   Three-Layer Cheesecake, 179
   Triple Layer Fudge Cake, 173
   Tropical Banana Cake, 161
   White Chocolate Tart, 151
   Yam Pecan Pie, 170
Dressings (see salad dressings)

F

Fish
   Ahi with Tomatillo-Apple Relish, 114
   Orange Roughy, Herb Broiled, 111
   Oriental Swordfish, 130
   Salmon with Red Pepper Sauce, 98
   Seabass with Chipotle Lime Sauce, 124
   Sole Florentine, 112
   Tropical Grilled, 102
   Trout, Smoked, Fettucine, 103

Index

Flan, 174
Flour Tortillas, 58
French Bread, 55
French Silk Pie, 163
Fruit
    Fruit, Nut & Vegetable Bread, 66
    Scones, 54
    Smoothies, 16

G
Gazpacho, 36
Green Sauce, Mexican, 70
Guacamole, 24

H,I
Hazelnut Biscotti, 133
Hazelnut Torte, Chocolate, 178
Herb Broiled Orange Roughy, 111
Herb Rolls, 48
Honey Mustard Dressing, 73
Huevos, 19
Hummus Pita Sandwiches, 119
Icing
    Cream Cheese, 168
    Chocolate, 173

K,L
Key Lime Pie, 155
Kiwi-Lime Vinaigrette, 73
Lasagna, Vegetable, 106
Lemon Cheese Pie, Lowfat, 150
Lentil Soup, 33
Linguine with Chile Pesto, 120

M
Mahogany Chicken, 121
Marinated Greens, 92
Marinated Shrimp & Vegetable Salad, 83
Meatloaf, 123
Mexican
    Breakfast Burritos, 17
    Chicken Quesadillas, 97
    Chile Con Queso, 27
    Chile Verde Soup, 35
    Chilequiles, 99
    Cornbread, 52
    Enchilada Sauce, 74
    Enchiladas, 94
    Flour Tortillas, 58
    Gazpacho, 36
    Guacamole, 24
    Huevos, 19
    Nachos, 28

    Navajo Tacos, 96
    Rice, 86
    Salsa, 69
    Tamale Pie, 95
    Tomatillo Sauce, 70
    Tortilla Soup, 34
Mousse, Chocolate, 172
Muffins
    Banana Walnut, 51
    Blueberry, 60
    Bran, 61
    Pumpkin Date, 62
    Pumpkin Oatbran, 63
Mushroom Soup, Cream of, 38

N,O
Nachos, 28
Navajo Tacos, 96
Oatmeal
    Chocolate Chip Cookies, 132
    Cookies, 142
    Fudge Cake, 157
Orange Roughy, Herb Broiled, 111
Oriental Noodle Salad, 82
Oriental Swordfish, 130

P
Pachos, 21
Pancakes
    Buttermilk, 20
    Sourdough, 18
    Zucchini Potato, 91
Parmesan Chicken, 116
Parmesan Potato Sticks, 90
Pasta
    Linguine with Smoked Chicken & Chile Pesto, 120
    Oriental Noodle Salad, 82
    Pesto, 115
    Primavera Asiago, 110
    Smoked Trout Fettucine, 103
    Tortellini with Proscuitto Cream, 108
    Vegetable Lasagna, 106
Peach Blueberry Crisp, 147
Peanut Butter Cookies, 143
Peanut Butter Pie, 149
Peanut Sauce, 29
Pecans (see desserts)
Pesto Potato Salad, 81
Pies
    Apple Caramel, 171
    Chocolate Banana Split, 152
    Chocolate Bourbon Pecan, 154

Index

Chocolate Chip, 165
Chocolate Dream, 164
Crust, 150
French Silk, 163
Key Lime, 155
Lowfat Lemon Cheese, 150
Peanut Butter, 149
Pecan, 166
Pumpkin, 156
Raspberry Cream, 175
Yam Pecan, 170
Pineapple Cheesecake, 176
Poppy Seed Dressing, 72
Pork
    Barbecued, Sandwiches, 122
    Medallions in Mustard Sauce, 118
Potatoes
    and Carrots in Cream, 84
    Caraway Bread, 65
    Cheese Soup, 39
    Pachos, 21
    Parmesan Potato Sticks, 90
    Roasted Rosemary, 87
    Salad, Pesto, 81
    Sweet, Pureé, 88
    Twice Baked, 85
    Zucchini Pancakes, 91
Pumpkin
    Date Muffins, 62
    Oatbran Muffins, 63
    Pie, 156

R

Raspberry
    Bars, 139
    Cream Pie, 175
    Vinaigrette, 72
Relishes
    Avocado, 68
    Tomatillo-Apple, 114
    Tropical, 102
Rice
    Pilaf, Vegetable, 89
    Mexican, 86
Roasted Rosemary Potatoes, 87
Rolls, Herb, 48

S

Salads
    Bean, Mixed, 78
    Caesar, 80
    Coleslaw, 79
    Marinated Greens, 92

Oriental Noodle, 82
Potato, Pesto, 81
Shrimp & Vegetable, Marinated, 83
Salad Dressings
    Caesar, 80
    Carrot Sesame, 75
    Chutney, 76
    Honey Mustard, 73
    Kiwi Lime, 73
    Lemon Caper, 92
    Poppy Seed, 72
    Raspberry Vinaigrette, 72
    Sundried Tomato Vinaigrette, 71
Salmon with Roasted Red Pepper Sauce, 98
Salsa, 69
Sandwiches
    Barbecued Pork, 122
    Cajun Chicken, 126
    Hummus Pita, 119
    Spinach Burger, 128
    Turkey Tarragon Burger, 129
Sauces
    Banana, 30
    Barbecue, 122
    Chipotle Lime,, 124
    Curry, 30
    Enchilada, 74
    Green Chile Pesto, 120
    Jalapeño, 30
    Mustard Cream, 118
    Orange Mustard, 125
    Oriental, 130
    Peanut, 229
    Pesto, 115
    Proscuitto Cream, 108
    Roasted Red Pepper, 98
    Salsa, 69
    Tomatillo, 70
    Tomatillo-Apple Relish, 114
    Tomato Cream, 106
    Tropical, 102
Scallops, Stirfried with Greens, 104
Scones
    Corn Cheese, 53
    Fruit, 54
Seabass with Lime Chipotle Sauce, 124
Seafood Bisque, 43
Sesame Chicken, 113
Shortbread Cookies, 138
Shrimp
    & Vegetable Salad, Marinated, 83
    with Peanut Sauce, Spicy, 29

Index

Side Dishes
    Mexican Rice, 86
    Parmesan Potato Sticks, 90
    Pesto Potato Salad, 81
    Potatoes & Carrots in Cream, 84
    Rice Pilaf, Vegetable, 89
    Roasted Rosemary Potatoes, 87
    Sweet Potato Pureé, 88
    Twice Baked Potatoes, 85
    Zucchini Potato Pancakes, 91
Smoked Trout Fettucine, 103
Smoothies, 16
Sole Florentine, 112
Soups
    Chicken Tortellini, 40
    Chile Verde, 35
    Corn Chowder, 46
    Cream of Asparagus, 32
    Cream of Chicken with Green Chiles, 41
    Cream of Mushroom, 38
    Creamy Dijon Chicken, 42
    Gazpacho, 36
    Potato Cheese, 39
    Seafood Bisque, 43
    Split Pea, 37
    Tortilla, 34
    Vegetarian Lentil, 33
Sour Cream Coffee Cake, 64
Sourdough
    Biscuits, 50
    Pancakes, 18
    Starter, 49
Southwestern Chicken Kiev, 105
Spanakopita, 109
Spinach Burgers, 128
Split Pea Soup, 37
Stew, Beef, 127
Stirfried Scallops and Greens, 104
Sundried Tomato Vinaigrette, 71
Sweet Potato Pureé, 88
Swordfish, Oriental, 130

T

Tacos, Navajo, 96
Tamale Pie, 95
Tomato Beef Chowmein, 117
Tomatillo-Apple Relish, 114
Tomatillo Sauce, 70
Tortellini Soup, and Chicken, 40
Tortellini with Proscuitto Cream Sauce, 108
Tortilla Soup, 34
Tortillas, Flour, 58
Triple Chunk Cookies, 144

Tropical Banana Cake, 161
Tropical Grilled Fish, 102
Turkey Scramble, Lowfat, 22
Turkey Tarragon Burgers, 129
Turtle Bars, 135
Twice Baked Potatoes, 85

V,W

Vegetable Rice Pilaf, 89
Vegetables, Marinated with Shrimp, 83
Vegetarian (also see Mexican, Soups, Pasta)
    Chili, 44
    Hummus Pitas, 119
    Lasagna, 106
    Spanakopita, 109
    Spinach Burgers, 128
White Chocolate
    Tart, 151
    Triple Chunk Cookies, 144
Wheat Germ Cookies, 140
Whole Wheat Sourdough Pancakes, 18

Y,Z

Yam Pecan Pie, 170
Zucchini Potato Pancakes, 91
Zucchini, Fruit & Nut Bread, 66

To: Dudley's
P.O. Box 6368
Snowmass Village, Colorado 81615

Please send me _____ copies of Food With A View at $13.95 each ($11.95 plus shipping).

Enclosed is my check for _____

    Ship to:

    _____

    _____

    _____

To: Dudley's
P.O. Box 6368
Snowmass Village, Colorado 81615

Please send me _____ copies of Food With A View at $13.95 each ($11.95 plus shipping).

Enclosed is my check for _____

    Ship to:

    _____

    _____

    _____